NATIONAL ACADEMIES

Sciences
Engineering
Medicine

NATIONAL
ACADEMIES
PRESS
Washington, DC

Structural Racism and Rigorous Models of Social Inequity

Linda Casola, *Rapporteur*

Committee on Population

Division of Behavioral and
Social Sciences and Education

T0003511

Proceedings of a Workshop

THE NATIONAL ACADEMIES PRESS 500 Fifth Street, NW Washington, DC 20001

This activity was supported by the National Institutes of Health (Award # HSN263201800029I-75N98021F00013). Any opinions, findings, conclusions, or recommendations expressed in this publication do not necessarily reflect the views of any organization or agency that provided support for the project.

International Standard Book Number-13: 978-0-309-69281-6
International Standard Book Number-10: 0-309-69281-4
Digital Object Identifier: https://doi.org/10.17226/26690

This publication is available from the National Academies Press, 500 Fifth Street, NW, Keck 360, Washington, DC 20001; (800) 624-6242 or (202) 334-3313; http://www.nap.edu.

Copyright 2022 by the National Academy of Sciences. National Academies of Sciences, Engineering, and Medicine and National Academies Press and the graphical logos for each are all trademarks of the National Academy of Sciences. All rights reserved.

Printed in the United States of America.

Suggested citation: National Academies of Sciences, Engineering, and Medicine. (2022). *Structural Racism and Rigorous Models of Social Inequity: Proceedings of a Workshop*. Washington, DC: The National Academies Press. https://doi.org/10.17226/26690.

The **National Academy of Sciences** was established in 1863 by an Act of Congress, signed by President Lincoln, as a private, nongovernmental institution to advise the nation on issues related to science and technology. Members are elected by their peers for outstanding contributions to research. Dr. Marcia McNutt is president.

The **National Academy of Engineering** was established in 1964 under the charter of the National Academy of Sciences to bring the practices of engineering to advising the nation. Members are elected by their peers for extraordinary contributions to engineering. Dr. John L. Anderson is president.

The **National Academy of Medicine** (formerly the Institute of Medicine) was established in 1970 under the charter of the National Academy of Sciences to advise the nation on medical and health issues. Members are elected by their peers for distinguished contributions to medicine and health. Dr. Victor J. Dzau is president.

The three Academies work together as the **National Academies of Sciences, Engineering, and Medicine** to provide independent, objective analysis and advice to the nation and conduct other activities to solve complex problems and inform public policy decisions. The National Academies also encourage education and research, recognize outstanding contributions to knowledge, and increase public understanding in matters of science, engineering, and medicine.

Learn more about the National Academies of Sciences, Engineering, and Medicine at **www.nationalacademies.org.**

Consensus Study Reports published by the National Academies of Sciences, Engineering, and Medicine document the evidence-based consensus on the study's statement of task by an authoring committee of experts. Reports typically include findings, conclusions, and recommendations based on information gathered by the committee and the committee's deliberations. Each report has been subjected to a rigorous and independent peer-review process and it represents the position of the National Academies on the statement of task.

Proceedings published by the National Academies of Sciences, Engineering, and Medicine chronicle the presentations and discussions at a workshop, symposium, or other event convened by the National Academies. The statements and opinions contained in proceedings are those of the participants and are not endorsed by other participants, the planning committee, or the National Academies.

Rapid Expert Consultations published by the National Academies of Sciences, Engineering, and Medicine are authored by subject-matter experts on narrowly focused topics that can be supported by a body of evidence. The discussions contained in rapid expert consultations are considered those of the authors and do not contain policy recommendations. Rapid expert consultations are reviewed by the institution before release.

For information about other products and activities of the National Academies, please visit www.nationalacademies.org/about/whatwedo.

PLANNING COMMITTEE FOR A WORKSHOP ON STRUCTURAL
RACISM AND RIGOROUS MODELS OF SOCIAL INEQUITY

HEDWIG (HEDY) LEE (*Chair*), Duke University
RENÉ D. FLORES, University of Chicago
MARGARET T. HICKEN, University of Michigan
TREVON D. LOGAN, The Ohio State University
JENNIFER J. MANLY, Columbia University
DAVID T. TAKEUCHI, University of Washington

Staff

MALAY K. MAJMUNDAR, *Study Director*
JOSHUA LANG, *Senior Program Assistant*

COMMITTEE ON POPULATION

ANNE R. PEBLEY (*Chair*), University of California, Los Angeles
EMILY M. AGREE, The Johns Hopkins University
DEBORAH BALK, City University of New York
ANN K. BLANC, The Population Council (retired)
COURTNEY C. COILE, Wellesley College
SONALDE DESAI, University of Maryland
DANA A. GLEI, Georgetown University
ROBERT A. HUMMER, The University of North Carolina, Chapel Hill
HEDWIG (HEDY) LEE, Duke University
TREVON D. LOGAN, The Ohio State University
JENNIFER J. MANLY, Columbia University
JENNA NOBLES, University of Wisconsin–Madison
FERNANDO RIOSMENA, University of Colorado Boulder
DAVID T. TAKEUCHI, University of Washington

Staff

MALAY K. MAJMUNDAR, *Director*

Acknowledgments

This document summarizes the discussions and presentations at the Workshop on Structural Racism and Rigorous Models of Social Inequity. Held as a hybrid meeting in Washington, DC, on May 16–17, 2022, the workshop was convened by the Committee on Population of the National Academies of Sciences, Engineering, and Medicine, and it was sponsored by the National Institute on Aging.

This Proceedings has been prepared by the workshop rapporteur as a factual summary of what occurred at the workshop. The planning committee's role was limited to planning and convening the workshop. The views contained in the proceedings are those of individual workshop participants and do not necessarily represent the views of all workshop participants, the planning committee, or the National Academies.

This Proceedings of a Workshop was reviewed in draft form by individuals chosen for their diverse perspectives and technical expertise. The purpose of this independent review is to provide candid and critical comments that will assist the National Academies of Sciences, Engineering, and Medicine in making each published proceedings as sound as possible and to ensure that it meets the institutional standards for quality, objectivity, evidence, and responsiveness to the charge. The review comments and draft manuscript remain confidential to protect the integrity of the process.

We thank the following individuals for their review of this proceedings: Hedwig Lee, Duke University. We also thank staff reader Kelly L. Robbins for reading and providing helpful comments on the proceedings manuscript.

Although the reviewers listed above provided many constructive comments and suggestions, they were not asked to endorse the content of the proceedings, nor did they see the final draft before its release. The review of this proceedings was overseen by Mark D. Hayward, University of Texas at Austin. He was responsible for making certain that an independent examination of this proceedings was carried out in accordance with the standards of the National Academies and that all review comments were carefully considered. Responsibility for the final content rests entirely with the rapporteur and the National Academies.

Malay K. Majmundar, *Director*
Committee on Population

Contents

Boxes and Figures

Acronyms and Abbreviations

AIAN   American Indian or Alaska Native

BSR   Division of Behavioral and Social Research

CARHE   Center for Antiracism Research for Health Equity

MRI   magnetic resonance imaging

NACA   National Advisory Council on Aging
NIA   National Institute on Aging
NIH   National Institutes of Health
NLSY   National Longitudinal Survey of Youth

SES   socioeconomic status

Introduction

Structural racism refers to the public and private policies, institutional practices, norms, and cultural representations that inherently create unequal freedom, opportunity, value, resources, advantage, restrictions, constraints, or disadvantage for individuals and populations according to their race and ethnicity both across the life course and between generations. Developing a research agenda on structural racism includes consideration of the historical and contemporary policies and other structural factors that explicitly or implicitly affect the health and well-being of individuals, families, and communities, as well as strategies to measure those factors.

The Committee on Population of the National Academies of Sciences, Engineering, and Medicine convened a two-day public workshop on May 16–17, 2022, to identify and discuss the mechanisms through which structural racism operates, with a particular emphasis on health and well-being; to develop an agenda for future research and data collection on structural racism; and to strengthen the evidence base for policy making (see Box I-1 for the workshop's statement of task and Appendix A for the workshop agenda). The workshop was sponsored by the National Institute on Aging (NIA) and an interdisciplinary steering committee was appointed by the National Academies to plan the structure and content. Invited speakers included investigators from relevant studies, population health researchers, and experts across disciplines with innovative methodologies. Speaker presentations and workshop discussions provided insights into known sources of structural racism and rigorous models of health inequity, revealed novel sources and approaches informed by other disciplines as well

1

BOX I-1
Statement of Task

A planning committee of the National Academies of Sciences, Engineering, and Medicine (with expertise in areas such as economics, epidemiology, psychology, public health, and sociology) will plan and execute a two-day public workshop that will bring together an interdisciplinary group of researchers and other relevant stakeholders to identify and discuss the sources and mechanisms through which structural racism operates. The workshop will address: how structural racism contributes to health inequities by race and ethnicity; the degree to which structural health inequities are explained by place-based factors and historical and contemporary experiences/exposures unique to people of color (e.g., immigration, segregation, incarceration, health care); the data and methods that are needed to further study these topics, such as measuring structural racism; and policy and other interventions at different levels (e.g., individual, family, community) that are needed to alleviate health inequities. After the workshop, proceedings of a workshop of the presentations and discussions at the workshop will be prepared by a designated rapporteur in accordance with institutional guidelines.

as related fields, and highlighted key research and data priorities for future work on structural racism and health inequity.

FOUNDATION OF THE WORKSHOP

Frank Bandiera (program officer in the Division of Behavioral and Social Research [BSR] at NIA) explained that the first recommendation from the 2019 review of BSR by the National Advisory Council on Aging (NACA) had to do with health disparities. Specifically, the NACA review noted that "the shocking extent of growing SES [socioeconomic status] and regional differences in mortality and life expectancy, as well as persistent racial inequalities, have been documented, and increasing understanding of the sources and approaches to ameliorating these needs [are] to be a major research focus going forward" (National Institute on Aging and National Advisory Council on Aging, 2019, p. 4). The review encouraged researchers to move past the documentation of differences and toward an improved understanding of the sources of the differences and of approaches to ameliorate them.

Bandiera said that as a first step, NIA asked the Committee on Population to host a virtual seminar in May 2020 titled "Persistent and Large

Racial/Ethnic Disparities: Beyond the Role of Socioeconomic Status,"[1] at which several topics were discussed: the role of race and ethnicity in U.S. health disparities; poor health outcomes related to life-course stress from racism, discrimination, and other exposures; and the connection between intergenerational mobility and racial/ethnic disparities, with particular emphasis on immigration. NIA sponsored the Workshop on Structural Racism and Rigorous Models of Social Inequity as a follow-on to the May 2020 seminar, Bandiera explained, with recognition of increasing demand for the following:

1. More rigorous models of social inequity in poor health outcomes to inform policy at the national, state, and local levels;
2. Intersectional research to understand the multidimensional effects of racism on racial/ethnic minority subgroups;
3. Enhanced data infrastructure for developing validated measures of health among racial/ethnic minorities, for implementing effective survey techniques that avoid self-selection bias, for coding historical data to measure racism, and for incorporating longitudinal studies in the analysis of relationships; and
4. Better understanding of the complexity of how racism is expressed.

Hedwig (Hedy) Lee (workshop planning committee chair and professor of sociology at Duke University) pointed out that the term *structural racism* is now used often in the media, by politicians, and across the population health sciences. She noted that in population health studies there are efforts to measure and model structural racism as a social determinant of health, which continues to expand. Lee reflected on a previous discussion with Kathleen Mullan Harris, professor of sociology at the University of North Carolina at Chapel Hill, about the integration of biological and social information in population health research. Harris cautioned population health scientists to avoid becoming distracted by "new and shiny" data, such as biomarkers, and to avoid producing "simplistic, sound-bite research" that could actually move the field backward.

Lee emphasized that although the study of structural racism might be relatively new for many population health researchers, the concept of structural racism is not—it is foundational in the United States and across the world, as well as the practices of genocide, colonization, and slavery. These practices have been "justified through moral and cultural arguments" that permeate everyday life in ways that are often difficult to observe. Quoting Eduardo Bonilla-Silva (James B. Duke distinguished professor of sociology

---

[1] https://www.nationalacademies.org/event/05-18-2020/cpop-seminar-seminar-on-persistent-and-large-racial-ethnic-disparities-beyond-the-role-of-socoieconomic-status-ses

at Duke University), Lee noted that racism "is in the air we breathe." Racism is part of the landscape of the United States—the District of Columbia itself was built by slaves and stolen from Native people. Further, when Thomas Jefferson wrote "all men are created equal," she continued, Black Americans and Native Americans were excluded.

Lee commented that, given this context, population health researchers cannot overlook insights on structural racism from other disciplines—for example, scholars in the humanities, history, and the social sciences have been documenting structural racism for more than a century. She suggested that population health researchers use these insights to inform the measurement and modeling of structural racism and to create linkages to health across the life course, which will ensure that their work has the potential both to contribute to improved population health and well-being and to reduce disparities.

Lee stressed that no individual scholar, workshop, or discipline can describe, measure, or model structural racism completely. Structural racism research is best approached with collaboration across disciplines. Lee invited speakers and participants to consider the following key question throughout the workshop: how can insights be applied regarding the conceptualization, measurement, and modeling of structural racism to inform decisions about:

1. What new measures of structural racism or data linkages could be used in ongoing or future studies helpful to advance aging research;
2. What mechanisms or data linkages could be used in ongoing or future studies that link structural racism to disparities in health and well-being over time and place; and
3. What study designs could be used to consider how structural factors operate to shape health over the life course?

ORGANIZATION OF THIS PROCEEDINGS

Chapter 1 offers foundational definitions for and discussions of the responsible study of race and structural racism—drawn primarily from the humanities and humanistic social sciences—and highlights the value of understanding the complexity of these concepts and applying them to data collection and analysis in an effort to improve health and well-being and to reduce health disparities. Chapter 2 describes measurement and modeling approaches for the study of structural racism, with specific attention toward the strengths and weaknesses of these approaches for population health and aging research. Chapter 3 summarizes expert insights on data and data infrastructure needs both to measure and model structural racism and to identify and measure the mechanisms that link racism to population health and well-being over time. Chapter 4 presents key takeaways from the workshop presentations and discussions, with an emphasis on the path forward.

This Proceedings follows the general structure of the workshop and has been prepared by the workshop rapporteur as a factual summary of what occurred at the workshop. The workshop planning committee's role was limited to organizing and convening the workshop (see Appendix B for biographical sketches of the workshop discussants and speakers). The views expressed in this proceedings are those of the individual workshop participants and do not necessarily represent the views of the participants as a whole, the planning committee, or the National Academies.

1

Setting the Foundation: Studying Race and Structural Racism Responsibly

---

Key Points Highlighted by Presenters

- The use of narrative and metaphor is important for better understanding the complexities of race and lived experiences of racism. (Stephanie Li)
- The study of structural racism is complex given that race is continually being made and remade over time by custom, law, and scholarship. (Evelynn Hammonds)
- Thinking about racism only as a form of prejudice makes it impossible to understand the drivers of structural racism; instead, a theoretical understanding of the racialized social system would be beneficial. (Eduardo Bonilla-Silva)
- The key path forward in structural racism research centers on building interdisciplinary frameworks that integrate scholarship from the arts, humanities, social sciences, and population health. (Margaret Hicken)

Welcoming participants to the first session of the workshop, discussant Trevon Logan (workshop planning committee member and Hazel C. Youngberg distinguished professor of economics at The Ohio State University) observed the growing interest among population health researchers in understanding the effects of structural racism on material conditions and outcomes at particular points in time and throughout the life course. He emphasized the value of social scientists learning from humanists and humanistic social scientists about race, racism, race-making, and structural racism as dynamic processes.

RACE, RACE-MAKING, AND THE USE OF RACE TO CONTROL POPULATIONS

Use of Narrative and Metaphor

Presenter Stephanie Li (Lynne Cooper Harvey distinguished professor of English at Washington University in St. Louis) championed the use of narrative and metaphor to better understand the complexities of race, which she described as "a social construction that determines what many perceive as essential aspects of identity" and that influences how individuals exist and relate. Reflecting further on the meaning of race, she noted that race has been categorized as an ideology, a structure, a history, a community, and an identity; however, class, gender, sexuality, and nationality "collude with race to make an indelible mark of social difference [that is] just out of reach." She underscored that race remains the most important determinant of life outcomes, such as residence, salary, and life expectancy.

Given the difficulty of defining race, Li explored several insightful metaphors presented by literary scholars. For instance, she indicated that James Baldwin (1984) described Whiteness as a form of blindness to the violent history that "branded its inequalities" into the nation's landscape. In *Invisible Man*, Ralph Ellison (1952) portrayed Black subjectivity as a "condition of invisibility." Claudia Rankine (2015) compared Black life to a "condition of mourning" in a world in which a person can be killed for being Black. In other words, Li explained, Blackness "is inextricable from the imminent possibility of death . . . and is to live without shelter." She also described the work of Edwidge Danticat (2016), who compared Black people in the United States to refugees, "as though [they] were members of a group in transit . . . who should either die or go somewhere else." Li remarked that although these metaphors do not fully capture the complexities of race, they offer "modes of understanding" that reveal the injustices of the world, as all of these perspectives connect Black life to a lack of safety, as well as to a "systematic devaluation." She emphasized that data on incarceration, the achievement gap, housing inequalities, and health disparities are readily available to support such narratives.

Asserting that racism infects all aspects of life, Li shared examples of the ways in which people communicate the danger and anxiety associated with race. For example, Ta-Nehisi Coates (2015) recounts being unable to enjoy an evening with a new friend because he was anticipating an attack that did not occur, in part because his "eyes were made in Baltimore . . . blindfolded by fear." Li described Coates's inability to be comfortable with a White stranger, even though he was never in danger, as an ingrained "anticipatory stress response," having been taught that all White people pose a threat to Black people in a city that was segregated and violent, with poor educational and job opportunities. Li underscored that the inability to trust a White person is the "cost of the vigilance required to exist" as a Black man in the United States; therefore, Coates's narrative reveals the detrimental consequences of structural racism on basic human relationships. However, Coates's writings on President Barack Obama describe a different experience with trust; the "kinds of traumas that marked African Americans of his generation . . . were mostly abstract for him" (Coates, 2017), owing to a different upbringing. Coates suggested that President Obama trusted White America, unlike many African Americans, who are "too crippled by [their] defenses" (Coates, 2017)—the same defenses that enable survival, Li observed.

In closing, Li explained that although racism begins in history and policy, it "resides in our bodies and our eyes." She recalled Toni Morrison's (1998) envisioning of race as a physical structure—a house—that defines the landscape and threatens to restrict movement. However, instead of escaping, Morrison aimed to transform this structure from "a windowless prison into which I was forced" to "an open house, grounded, yet generous in its supply of windows and doors" and further to "an out of doors safety where a 'sleepless woman . . . could walk out the yard and on down the road. No lamp and no fear'" (Morrison, 1998, p. 4, 10). Li indicated that this freedom of movement symbolizes the liberation of race (versus its containment), and that Morrison challenged people to rebuild the structures of their lives, anchored in the strength of community instead of restricted by the absence of safety.

How Race Is Made and Remade Over Time

Serving as the session's second presenter, Evelynn Hammonds (Barbara Gutmann Rosenkrantz professor of the history of science, professor of African and African American studies, and professor in the Department of Social and Behavioral Sciences at Harvard T.H. Chan School of Public Health, Harvard University) described her interest in historicized understandings of race and racism, as well as in the notion that race is continually being "made and remade" over time by custom, law, and scholarship.

Hammonds provided key definitions to introduce the concept of race and to frame the workshop's discussions of structural racism (see Box 1-1).

Reflecting on the murder of Michael Brown in Ferguson, Missouri as a case study in racecraft, Hammonds highlighted the flaws in the explanation that Brown was shot because he was Black, which "veil[s] the work of multiple forms of racism that led a law enforcement official to shoot this young man to death. . . . Brown's blackness did not pull the trigger. . . . Brown was not shot because he was black. He is black because he was shot" (see Benjamin, 2014). In essence, "race is the result of the power some people

---

BOX 1-1
Key Definitions

Race "stands for the conception or doctrine that nature produced human-kind in distinct groups, each defined by inborn traits that its members share and that differentiate them from members of other distinct groups of the same kind but of unequal rank" (Fields and Fields, 2012, p. 16). Quoting Barbara Johnson, professor of English at Harvard University, Hammonds explained that race is an "already read script": people make assumptions about others' character and culture based on their appearance, and that script has not changed in more than a century.

Racecraft is "an ongoing set of social practices that continuously mis-construe racism for race" (Benjamin, 2014).

Racism is "the theory and practice of applying a social, civic, or legal double standard based on ancestry, and to the ideology surrounding such a double standard" (Fields and Fields, 2012). Racism can also be described as a "function of power and inequality whereas race is purportedly grounded in biology and culture" (Benjamin, 2014). Racism is "not an emotion or state of mind, such as intolerance, bigotry, hatred, or malevolence"; it is a "social prac-tice, which means that it is an action and a rationale for action or both at once" (Fields and Fields, 2012).

---

have over others" (see Fields and Fields, 2012). Hammonds explained that the idea of inherent racial difference has continued to shape perceptions of race and articulations of these perceptions in contorted ways across centuries. Thus, understanding the historical nature of race and racism demands "map[ping] the relations of power, the patterns of contestation and struggle out of which such social constructions emerged" (see Holt, 2000). Hammonds reiterated that there is no single social construct of race.

Tracing historical discussions of race, Hammonds described W.E.B. Du Bois's contribution of 60 data visualizations in 1900 to an exhibit in Paris that focused on the progress of African Americans since Emancipation. One of these infographics, "Valuation of Town and City Property Owned by Georgia Negroes," plotted the value of property owned by African Americans from 1870 to 1900 within the context of political and socioeconomic events—the rise of the Ku Klux Klan in the 1870s; industrialism in the 1880s; and lynching, financial panic, and disenfranchisement in the 1890s. Property value increased until approximately 1900, at which point a decline began. This visualization prompts its viewers to consider the historical context in which African Americans acquired property:

[It] links the economic progress of black Georgians to larger regimes of violence against African Americans, pointing to the widespread disenfranchisement and dispossession of black people in the post-Reconstruction era . . . [and] illustrate[s] through evidence . . . how centuries of racial oppression and exploitation, not a lack of natural aptitude, had shaped the current abysmal conditions of black life world wide. (Battle-Baptiste and Rusert, 2018, p. 80)

Hammonds underscored that Du Bois collected data on a wide range of topics related to the actual lived experiences of African Americans in the context of a society that was structured by racial inequality and that reproduced this inequality over time. Du Bois addressed and raised problematic questions about race, even though society was not ready for this type of research at the time. Hammonds encouraged contemporary scholars to embrace Du Bois's model of structural racism, as such social data illuminate the structural components of how race and racism are made and remade over time.

EMBRACING THE COMPLEXITY OF STRUCTURAL RACISM AND UNDERSTANDING THE INTERLOCKING FEATURES OF CULTURAL AND STRUCTURAL RACISM

The Racialized Social System

Presenter Eduardo Bonilla-Silva (James B. Duke distinguished professor of sociology at Duke University) explained that, while the use of terms such as systemic racism and structural racism has increased, much of society still fails to recognize how racism is systemic. To illustrate the systemic nature of racism, he presented a brief analysis of the police force, beginning with its history as an extension of slave patrols. Currently, he continued, as an "agency of racial and social control," the police force chooses particular people to be officers and trains them in a racialized way, thus creating a "macho-military culture of 'us' versus 'them'" and steering officers to use race-based policing. According to Menifield and colleagues (2019), this "explains the seeming contradiction of officers of color being as likely as their White counterparts to use lethal force against people of color."

Bonilla-Silva indicated that this lack of understanding about the systemic nature of racism persists in part because society incorrectly conflates racism with prejudice. First, prejudice focuses on individuals' psychology or attitudes, whereas structural racism is collective and societal, and extends beyond attitude to create an ideology. Second, the notion of prejudice is ahistorical (i.e., assumes the racism of today is not different from that of yesteryears), whereas structural racism has a historical beginning, retains a set of practices that can change over time, and includes variations across locations. Third, prejudice is thought to revolve around overt actions, which neglects the common and covert ways that race matters. Lastly, prejudice focuses on the flawed morals of an individual, whereas structural racism has a material foundation (see Bonilla-Silva, 1997). Thus, he asserted that thinking about racism as a form of prejudice makes it impossible to understand the drivers of structural racism.

Although several alternative approaches to understanding structural racism exist, Bonilla-Silva emphasized the value of the "racialized social system" approach, which he developed in 1997. He explained that this theoretical framework is based on the following multidimensional premise: "the world-system was racialized in the 15th century, creating racialized social systems" in which "social, economic, political, and even psychological goods have been partially allocated by race." Furthermore, race and racism are "social and political constructs that are mutually reinforced." In other words, Bonilla-Silva continued, "race and racism coemerged and are codetermined." Although races are constructs, they are "socially real," he said, because belonging to the White race has positive consequences and belonging to a non-White race has negative consequences. As a result, races "develop different racial interests," with the subordinate groups challenging their position in the system and the dominant groups defending the racial order. This creates an opportunity for racial contestation, which is "the struggle for position in the racial order, which transpires infrequently through concerted collective action . . . but often through individuals' actions . . . or mostly through actors following the dominant racial script of a period" (see Bonilla-Silva, 1997). He stressed that any worthwhile structural theory of racism should recognize the collective practices and behaviors of members of a society; be both tied to history and cognizant of regional, local, and societal distinctions; be materialist; and consider individuals and their subjectivity, as well as how the racial structure is produced and reproduced.

Bonilla-Silva has further explored the complexity of structural racism and expanded the theory of the racialized social system in the years since his 1997 publication (see Bonilla-Silva, 2021). He explained that because "regular White folks" are fundamental to the maintenance of the racial order, understanding the "collective manufacture of Whiteness" is critical. He noted that the "White Habitus" molds individual Whites into Whiteness— the "hypersegregation" of White life (e.g., in residences, churches, friendships) reinforces Whiteness as a set of norms, culture, aesthetics, emotions, and cognitions (Bonilla-Silva, 2019, 2022). The Whiteness produced by this White Habitus, he continued, has become systemic. He underscored, however, that the "production of Whiteness and Blackness is always contingent"; in addition to being racialized, people are categorized by class, gender, sexual orientation, political orientation, education, and levels of interaction, which affects their "racial sensibilities." Therefore, Bonilla-Silva remarked that collective action through racial contestation is crucial to enable fundamental structural and cultural change.

Bonilla-Silva also described how understanding the systemic nature and historical context of racism is key to the methods and indicators society uses. For example, he discussed how an interpretation of residential segregation is based mostly on the index of residential dissimilarity[1] and the index of isolation. Using these indices to study racial segregation in neighborhoods, Vigdor and Glaeser (2012) revealed a decline in residential segregation since its peak in 1970. However, Bonilla-Silva emphasized that much progress remains to be made; although historical segregation patterns are beginning to change, they are changing because of gentrification, which only creates different realities within the same space. As an example, he portrayed Durham, North Carolina, as a city in which "whitopia" still dominates in places where Black and White people cohabitate spatially. In closing, Bonilla-Silva provided the following guidance to researchers conducting analyses of residential structural racism:

1. Because context and history matter, do not reify metrics;
2. Recognize that spaces and organizations are racialized;
3. Measure interracial contacts and their valence;
4. Examine (instead of assume) racial life in spaces such as neighborhoods (see Mayorga-Gallo, 2014); and
5. Consider power dynamics and the implications of arguments.

Defining and Measuring Cultural and Structural Racism

Serving as the final presenter of the session, Margaret Hicken (workshop planning committee member and research associate professor in the Institute for Social Research at the University of Michigan) explored how racism has been understood, measured, and modeled in population health and aging research, as well as how this aligns with conceptualizations of racism. She underscored that interdisciplinary scholarship—integrating research from the arts, humanities, and social sciences into population health research—creates stronger science, especially because public health and biomedical training are often misaligned with the reality of how structural racism shapes health and well-being. Reflecting on how researcher bias can influence this scholarship, she noted that racially diverse research teams are also highly beneficial. She emphasized, drawing from work by legal expert

---

[1] The index of residential dissimilarity measures the evenness of population distribution in a geographical area.

Charles Lawrence, that those with White privilege are often blind to the ways that structural racism affects population health, while scholars without White privilege have key insights about racialized processes. Without these diverse research collaborations, she cautioned, researchers cannot fully understand the processes they intend to measure—and science will not move forward.

Hicken expanded on the definitions of racism offered earlier in the workshop, first sharing philosopher Achille Mbembe's (2003) interpretation that racism is "a technology aimed at permitting the exercise of biopower"—the tool that allows society to "regulate the distribution of death." More specifically, Hicken described *cultural racism* as the socially accepted values, ideologies, and norms of a racialized society that are determined by the dominant power group. Cultural racism operates in the shared social subconscious and determines assumptions about who and what are important—that is, it shapes the answers to questions: Whose life counts? Who is fully American? Who deserves to live a long and healthy life? She explained that cultural racism also "acts as a distortion lens that renders racialized and racially hierarchical institutions neutral and rational." Thus, Hicken continued, *structural racism* is the application of cultural racism; the social structure is composed of formal and informal interrelated institutions, and that when attempts are made to achieve equity in one institution, other institutions intervene to restore the White privilege set up by cultural racism. Furthermore, she indicated that society's institutions "adapt to contemporaneous sociopolitical norms." These institutional shifts will be replaced by others in a more civilized way of killing, according to Mbembe (2003), if the underlying cultural racism does not change. Hicken underscored that historical race-based policies continue to influence current policies because structural racism "includes the erasure of historical processes that could clarify the link between racialized groups and health."

Turning to a discussion and evaluation of three specific strategies to measure and link cultural and structural racism, Hicken first depicted an approach that leverages individual-level reports and information—for example, reports of interpersonal prejudice or discrimination, anticipatory and perseverative thoughts and behaviors, beliefs about external regard for racialized groups, area-level composition of individual-level reports, skin tone, and documentation status. This type of information can be collected easily through interviews but is not meant to be a proxy for cultural or structural racism. She emphasized that these measures require a theory and a framework on how the constructs relate to cultural and structural racism within a particular context. Although each type of individual-level measure could be useful and could reveal possible connections between race and health, she continued, it is important to avoid mischaracterization of the measures, whose linkages to race and racism vary over time and place.

Hicken next described an approach that relies on multi-item indices, which are created by combining indicators in different ways to capture a construct. She asserted that an index significantly reduces the available information about constructs such as cultural and structural racism. For example, the critical information for a universal index of structural racism would be limited to a small number of formal institutions for which administrative data at a predetermined spatial level are available, by many unsubstantiated assumptions about the ways in which the components operate together over place and time, and with a narrow snapshot of contemporary life. These indices are difficult to interpret, she remarked, and thus create associations with health that are difficult to interpret. In some cases, the creation of indices may be useful in facilitating particular research questions, but she cautioned that indices are not indicators of structural racism.

Hicken commented that the field is moving toward more frequent use of an approach that captures specific features to better understand cultural and structural racism at local levels, both spatially and temporally—for example, via racial segregation (global and local residential, historical residential redlining, educational, and occupational); contemporary racial terror, surveillance, and control (police killings, mass incarceration, fines, and fees; child protective services; and vigilantism); and historical racial terror, surveillance, and control (mob violence, lynchings, enslavement, confederate monuments, Ku Klux Klan activity, and Jim Crow-era governance).

Hicken summarized that the key path forward for structural racism research centers on building interdisciplinary frameworks by integrating scholarship from the arts, humanities, social sciences, and population health; shifting away from atheoretical tests of racial group comparisons; and allowing for dynamic interactions among institutions. Further, underlying these frameworks and tests is the assumption that society is not moving toward equity. She championed the value of matching measurement and modeling to theory by reducing the use of universal, static, and temporally narrow indices; developing measures that reflect the spatially and temporally local nature of racism; embracing modeling approaches that allow for dynamic feedback loops and interactions among institutions over place and time; integrating historical information that could capture unmeasured or unmeasurable information about contemporary structures; and focusing on what information is actually captured by a measure, no matter what the measure may be labeled. She reiterated the value of creating diverse working groups and then challenged the current definition of academic success that privileges publishing alone or as lead author to achieve tenure and promotion, and the practice of waiting to discuss structural racism until tenured.

REFLECTIONS AND DISCUSSION

Continuing to serve as the session's discussant, Logan expressed his support for Hicken's assertion that scholarship from the humanities and the humanistic social sciences be integrated into population health and quantitative social science studies of structural racism—this interdisciplinary research could strengthen the theories that support the measures used as proxies for structural racism. He added that, because social science is ahistorical by nature, historians offer key insights into race as a dynamic process, as well as how people have understood race over time and place.

Logan offered further reflections on the first session of the workshop and on the topic of structural racism more broadly. He recalled sociologist Dorothy Roberts's understanding of race as a political construct, which focuses on the division of resources among people through the political process, and noted that this definition captures another aspect of the complexity of structural racism because it reveals how race is operationalized at the individual and institutional levels, where power dynamics reign. Lastly, he noted that because individuals define themselves relative to other individuals, a relational process would help to better understand structural racism.

Opening the general discussion, Logan posed the following question: What makes the social construct of race real? Hammonds explained that because the United States was defined by the exclusion of various people from the body politic, "social" and "political" constructs have not been and cannot be separated. Furthermore, she continued, the biological component of race underlies both the social and political constructs of race. She referred to a letter that W.E.B. Du Bois received from a White physician in 1906 asking if "the Negro shed tears," which illuminates the fact that meaning always has to be considered in context—there is no one way to define a social (or political) construct.

Logan wondered how to interrogate the data used to build measures that could capture structural racism. Hicken replied that the first step is to develop a research framework shaped by the arts, humanities, and social sciences. She noted that existing data are racialized, and researchers have access to a limited set of data—without a research framework, these data are difficult to interpret accurately. Next, she continued, researchers could use this framework to consider what the data have captured to better understand what is being measured and to create more appropriate research questions.

Frank Edwards (assistant professor of criminal justice at Rutgers University) described research from postcolonial theorists that reveals gaps in archives, which lead to gaps in the understanding of the forces that structure contemporary outcomes. Furthermore, he pointed out that data collection is an "activity of power"; for instance, official statistics on police violence in the United States do not exist. In the context of these gaps in exposure to forms of structural racism, he asked how public health researchers could measure historical processes of structural racism more appropriately. Bonilla-Silva advocated for "undoing our silence" in the archives—for example on colonialism, genocide, and land expropriation in the United States. Jennifer Manly (workshop planning committee member and professor of neuropsychology at Columbia University) cautioned researchers against becoming too distracted by machine learning and artificial intelligence. More and better data are needed, she said, but when some data are missing and other data are imperfect, creative approaches help to better understand how structural racism operates.

Logan observed that measures of segregation are often focused on metropolitan areas, and he inquired about capturing geospatial aspects of systemic racism that might not align with existing theories. Bonilla-Silva suggested analyzing local racial formations to examine how the production of racial order varies depending on rural, urban, large, and small populations. He mentioned that understanding the "rules and regulations" that maintain racial order in a particular location are as important as having better metrics. In Latin America, for example, the historical racial order is stronger than in the United States, which explains in part why income and education data reveal that the gaps between White people and non-White people are slightly larger there than in the United States. He suggested developing new indices for these situations, as well as studying segregation in situ.

A participant posed a question about avoiding the use of measurements that reinforce White normativity and assimilation as solutions for anti-Black racism. Bonilla-Silva explained that the index that was useful 40–60 years ago is much less useful now in depicting the ways in which segregation matters. He suggested that instead of "hunting for racists," researchers could examine the "depth of Whiteness"; such new metrics could produce a more robust measurement of structural racism. Hicken noted that consideration for spatial resolution is essential. Once the measure and spatial resolution are matched to the time and place where the research question is being asked, she said, segregation can be understood as a tool of structural racism—public and private entities systematically invest in some people while disinvesting in others. She encouraged researchers to evaluate how they are measuring segregation, whether this matches with the theory, and at what level segregation, which depends on place and time, is happening. Once the locations of investment and disinvestment have been identified, she continued, it becomes possible to target policy accordingly. Logan added that because the most popular measures of segregation in the social sciences are based on income inequality, researchers could consider what to measure, in a geospatial sense, that would apply to an income distribution. He encouraged researchers to study segregation in rural areas, occupations, and schools moving forward.

Another participant asked whether intersectionality helps or hinders understanding of racism. Li responded that although intersectionality is critical to understanding the effects of racism, its presence also creates challenges when other forms of discrimination, such as sexism, classism, and ageism, cannot be isolated. Thus, intersectionality is valuable as an approach, she continued, but its impact is difficult to measure. Hammonds added that intersectionality is crucial, but different data (e.g., disaggregated data) would enhance understanding. For example, over the last 10 years, approximately 68 percent of women seeking abortions in Mississippi have been African American, but it is unclear why (Fadel, 2022). To understand this finding and ultimately to make related policy changes, the systemic forces affecting those women (e.g., lack of access to public transit, primary care, and health insurance) have to be understood first; if one wants to make possible safe and legal access to abortions, it is necessary to understand why the highest rates are happening for women of color. Logan pointed out that this example relates to the workshop's earlier discussion about Michael Brown, and Hammonds reiterated that context is essential to reveal the structures that, for instance, prompt a law enforcement officer to see a Black face and think that the person can be killed with minimal interrogation about the crime. If race is relational, she added, then questions arise about what it means for White people to be White, as well as about the structures that produce Whiteness.

Li returned to the question that began this discussion—why and how these social constructs exist—and explained that they exist because of the narratives that underpin American identity and the founding of the nation, which relate to the concept of "White innocence." She noted that all of the achievements in the United States are based on the foundation of freedom and the pursuit of happiness, which in reality are "built on mass exploitation and genocide and the plunder of bodies of color." She emphasized the importance of challenging this notion of White innocence and changing the narrative that Blackness equates to violence, abjection, and disposability.

2

Assessing the Landscape:
The Measurement and Modeling
of Structural Racism

Key Points Highlighted by Presenters

- Experimental design, which has long been used for psychology research and is used increasingly by sociologists, political scientists, and economists, is a valuable approach to better understand existing racial stereotypes and their social consequences. Although issues might arise in experimental design related to data quality, access, and analysis and replication standards, as well as data training, many of these can be addressed with more resources and better infrastructure. (René D. Flores)
- Quasi-experimental approaches are useful in the study of structural racism in that they allow for estimates of causal parameters that policy makers can interpret; for example, the current use of lethal force among the police is driven primarily by governmental and institutional decisions rather than by intractable structural factors. (Jamein P. Cunningham)
- The history and historical contexts of structural racism operate as a fundamental cause of disease; therefore, including historical indicators in analyses is essential. Historical data at both the spatial/community and individual levels have the potential to advance research in health and social equity. (Amy Kate Bailey)
- Understudied Indigenous populations that have been historically marginalized, underresourced, systematically excluded, and erased are reclaiming their data sovereignty by decolonizing data. (Desi Small-Rodriguez)
- Algorithms can be trained to perform better than humans and reduce bias in health care, but only if these algorithms learn from nature (i.e., patient experiences and health outcomes) and prioritize patient experience. (Ziad Obermeyer)
- The complexity of people's experience of structural racism can be better understood with the use of diverse mixed methods (quantitative and qualitative) to explicate a phenomenon about which there is limited information, to corroborate existing evidence, or to dispute existing evidence. (Paris "AJ" Adkins-Jackson)

19

- Connections to land and place are central to Indigenous frameworks for health and healing. (Michelle Johnson-Jennings)
- Although longitudinal social surveys are well-suited for exploring the mechanisms that produce racialized inequities in health and other outcomes, their use also entails theoretical, epistemological, and methodological challenges. (Courtney Boen)
- Novel data not only present new opportunities to measure state violence but also reveal the limits of official statistics. Building infrastructure for unofficial data collection can enable valuable research on structural racism. (Frank Edwards)

EXPERIMENTAL DESIGN

René D. Flores (workshop planning committee member and Neubauer Family assistant professor of sociology at the University of Chicago) explored the use of experimental methods to identify the most common racial stereotypes in the United States, as well as to better understand how the intersection of race, class, and gender shapes these stereotypes.

Flores explained that stereotypes are assumptions about a group's behavioral traits and capacities (Bobo et al., 2012) that reveal how race is made. As the "building blocks of racial difference," stereotypes illuminate the changing nature of ethnoracial boundaries (Lamont, 2009) and serve as a means of explaining social processes such as discrimination, harassment, and intergroup relations (Fiske and Neuberg, 1990; Jussim et al., 1996). However, he observed that much of the existing research on stereotypes has examined stereotype content deductively—typically using closed-ended formats (Bobo and Kluegel, 1991; Schachter, 2021). While some inductive open-ended exercises exist, they are typically collected on convenience samples (Karlins et al, 1969), and issues of external validity may arise. Furthermore, some stereotype content research suggests that the intersection between two stigmatized categories (e.g., race, class, and/or gender) could actually decrease stigma (Pedulla, 2014) and that when gender and ethnicity are combined, novel stereotypes could be created (Ghavami and Peplau, 2013). Flores described how he and his colleague, Michael Gaddis (University of California, Los Angeles), are approaching stereotype content research, with a fully inductive methodology for revealing existing stereotypes; a nationally representative sample of U.S. non-Hispanic White (White) adults, who play an important role in the formation of U.S. ethnoracial boundaries; and a framework to identify intersectional effects.

Flores echoed Margaret Hicken's (workshop planning committee member and research associate professor in the Institute for Social Research at the University of Michigan) assertion about the value of incorporating more theory into studies of structural racism. Currently, the social science field is guided primarily by two models for understanding social stereotypes. First, the stereotype content model suggests that competence and warmth are the two key dimensions of stereotype-making. In this model, high-status, powerful groups are perceived as competent but perhaps as having little warmth (Fiske et al., 2002). Second, the racial position model suggests that the key dimensions of stereotype-making relate to groups perceived as inferior or superior and foreign or native (Zou and Cheryan, 2017). To determine which model has greater relevance for racial stereotypes, Flores and Gaddis conducted interviews of 200 White adults, using Amazon's crowdsourcing platform MTurk. In an open-ended fashion, they asked participants to name one of the most common stereotypes of White people, Hispanic people, Black people, Asian people, men, women, lower-class people, and upper-class people. From these interviews, approximately 116 traits were identified for each group. Flores and Gaddis used this information to populate 44 different Wiki surveys on all possible combinations of race, gender, and class. Using the online survey platform Prolific, 1,450 White survey respondents voted 89 times for a total of 128,946 votes on 664 unique stereotypes. As people voted on the prevalence of common stereotypes (or added additional stereotypes), a ranked order of the most popular stereotypes was produced. Finally, a new survey experiment was designed for a nationally representative sample of 2,500 White adults using YouGov, in which each adult was randomly assigned to one of the 44 combinations of gender, class, and race, and determined their conformance to the 250 most popular stereotypes identified in the prior survey.

Flores remarked that using the stereotype content model, one would expect to find the most common existing racial stereotypes to include degrees of competence (e.g., confidence, independence, competitiveness, organization, and intelligence) and warmth (e.g., tolerance, friendliness, and sincerity). However, Flores and Gaddis found that such stereotypes were not very popular: mentions of competence and warmth accounted for about 10 percent of the stereotypes identified by the nationally representative sample of White people. Flores displayed the top 30 stereotypes for each ethnoracial group as defined by the survey participants. For example, they perceived other White people as high-status, privileged, rich, powerful, and native; Black people as monolingual, poor, welfare-dependent, and low status; Asian people as foreign, career-oriented, and intelligent; and Hispanic people as foreign, poor, and undocumented. The participants revealed consistently positive stereotypes about Asian people, which contradicts the premise of the stereotype content model that "competent" people are perceived to lack "warmth." Flores and Gaddis concluded that focusing only on the dimensions of competence and warmth would not account for the full social reality of racial stereotypes; the racial position model better accounts for the patterns identified in the data they collected about the most popular stereotypes (e.g., participants viewed White people as American and superior, Black people as American and inferior, Asian people as foreign and superior, and Hispanic people as foreign and inferior).

Flores and Gaddis also used this experiment to consider how the intersection of race, class, and gender shape stereotype content, and observed that racial stereotypes overlap with class and gender stereotypes (Figure 2-1). For example, the participants' stereotypes about White people often tended to overlap with stereotypes about upper-class people and stereotypes about men, and stereotypes about Black and Hispanic people were more likely to overlap with stereotypes about lower-class people. Questioning how the composition of stereotypes changes with different combinations of race, class, and gender, Flores and Gaddis discovered a different distribution of stereotypes for lower-class White people. Flores explained that a difference of the same magnitude in the distribution of stereotypes was not apparent for lower-class Black, Hispanic, and Asian people and that there was little effect of intersectionality was shown relative to the other groups regardless of the race, class, and gender combination.

In closing, Flores discussed the benefits of the racial position model, which offered significant explanatory power to understand the racial stereo-

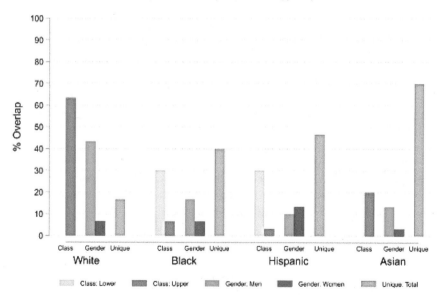

FIGURE 2-1 The overlap of racial stereotypes with class and gender stereotypes.
SOURCE: Workshop presentation by René D. Flores, May 16, 2022.

types content model. Additionally, although Flores and Gaddis's research revealed significant intersectional effects on stereotype content, the direction and magnitude of these effects depend on White participants' initial impressions of each ethnoracial group's socioeconomic status. Flores emphasized the value of using experimental design to observe the specific configurations of particular social situations, so as to better understand both the stereotypes that might be produced and their social consequences.

In response to a question from David Takeuchi (workshop planning committee member and professor and associate dean for faculty excellence in the University of Washington School of Social Work) about the method used for the experimental design survey, Flores explained that the experimental design survey was the final part of the data collection process. He noted that the reason for randomly assigning each participant to one of the 44 experimental conditions (which were derived from all possible combinations of race, class, and gender) was to reduce concerns about ocial desirability. This approach allowed Flores and Gaddis to estimate the experimental effects on individually reported stereotypes as a result of being assigned to each of the different conditions.

Hedwig (Hedy) Lee (workshop planning committee chair and professor of sociology at Duke University) asked about the future of experimental design. Flores replied that although experimental design has long been used for psychology research, sociologists, political scientists, and economists are beginning to build on that literature and engage more often with experimental methods—vast and inexpensive datasets are available online (e.g., via Prolific), and many questions can be explored with randomization. He cautioned that issues related to data quality, access, and analysis and replication standards, as well as registration standards and data training, might arise in experimental design, many of which could be addressed with more resources and a better infrastructure.

QUASI-EXPERIMENTAL APPROACHES

Jamein Cunningham (assistant professor in the Jeb E. Brooks School of Public Policy at Cornell University) provided an overview of the use of quasi-experimental research design for studying structural racism, particularly in relation to police use of lethal force. He noted that police violence is the leading cause of death for young Black males (Edwards et al., 2019), and in 2021, 1,051 Americans were killed by law enforcement officers—a disproportionate number of these Americans were from Black and Indigenous communities. Police violence is a growing concern not only in the United States but also in Europe and Canada.

Cunningham explained that recognizing and challenging structural racism first requires an understanding of the past. For example, the economic history community has long relied on quasi-experimental research design to study slavery, emancipation, and reconstruction (Conrad and Meyer, 1964; Fogel and Engerman, 1974; Ransom and Sutch, 1977); lynchings (Cook, 2014; Cook, Logan, and Parman, 2018); and segregation (Collins and Margo, 2003; Logan and Parman, 2017). He stressed that modern policing in the United States is related to the nation's complex history of race and discrimination. Slave patrols in the South were one of the first and most formal forms of American policing; furthermore, militias criminalized the behavior of former slaves after the Civil War, followed by state-sanctioned violence that directly or indirectly involved police (e.g., lynchings and White mob violence) (Chicago Commission on Race Relations, 1922; Lieberson and Silverman, 1965). Essentially, he continued, police departments opted to serve the White population.

To further illuminate the relationship between the past and the present, Cunningham described the positive relationship between the number of historical lynchings and the number of Black people killed by police, as well as the inverse relationship for White people (Williams and Romer, 2020). When testing this model to understand the persistence of this racial violence, Williams and colleagues (2022) found that places where lynchings occurred in the past have higher police violence today, as well as an increased intensity of racial violence more generally.

Cunningham remarked that emerging quasi-experimental and applied econometric scholarship can be used to understand the evolution of the use of lethal force in policing over time, the role of structural factors in determining the use of force, and the impact of policy interventions over time. He explained that data about police violence became more accessible in the 1950s and 1960s; however, deaths remained undercounted post-1960 (see Cunningham and Gillezeau, 2021; Figure 2-2). Several research studies have explored whether the increase in police killings of civilians in the 1960s could be attributed to structural, legal, or departmental factors. He emphasized that quasi-experimental methods are well-suited to study racial disparities in police violence and to isolate the effect because police violence is not random or conducted in a control environment, and these methods can exploit variation in exposure or treatment.

Reflecting on whether structural factors influence racial disparities in police violence, Cunningham mentioned that segregation has long been presumed to have driven the increase in use of lethal force in the 1960s. When Cox and colleagues (2022) tested the causal impact of segregation on victimization by using the index of dissimilarity and exploiting the historical layout of railroads, they found that segregation strongly predicts racial disparity in homicides; however, they were unable to link structural factors associated with poverty, inequality, and segregation to police killings of civilians in particular.

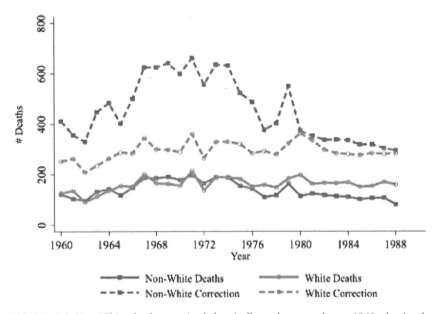

FIGURE 2-2 Non-White deaths remained drastically undercounted post-1960, despite the increased availability of data.
SOURCE: Cunningham and Gillezeau (2021).

To analyze legal factors that could influence racial disparities in police violence, Cunningham and colleagues (2021) exploited the variation between when/where police could not collectively bargain and when/where they first could. The researchers found that police killings of civilians began to increase 4–5 years after officers could collectively bargain (e.g., in the event of a killing of a civilian, police unions pay for and facilitate legal representation, meet with their member in advance of making a report, potentially facilitate a "huddling" of officers, and implement procedural protections during interrogation). Furthermore, they found that the introduction of bargaining rights for police increased the use of lethal force against non-White Americans by more than 70 percent, an increase that is not related to segregation or poverty.

Cunningham related that, to explore departmental factors that could influence racial disparities in police violence, Cox and colleagues (2021) exploited the variation in employment discrimination litigation against police departments in the 1970s and 1980s and found that racial diversity matters in police departments after a threat of affirmative action litigation, an effect that explains the relative decline in non-White deaths at the hands of police after 1970. Cunningham asserted that this is another example of the unrelated effect of structural factors, such as segregation, poverty, and inequality, demonstrating that police can change their behavior to reduce police violence.

Cunningham observed that the use of lethal force entered a relatively stable period with an upward trend in 1980, including a surge for non-White populations after 2000 and for White populations after 2008. This surge can be partially explained by militarization (Masera, 2021), force size and engagement (Goel et al., 2016), polarization and racial bias, and increases in violence and the drug trade (Holz et al., 2019). Cunningham and Stuart (2022) exploited variation in time and intensity of the Great Recession but found that the post-2008 surge in lethal force could not be explained by structural factors such as the related labor market outcomes. Even though the causes of this surge are not fully explainable, he continued, strong causal evidence exists for several mitigating factors: new technology (e.g., the efficacy of body cameras; see Williams et al., 2021), increased oversight and human resources (e.g., procedural justice training [Owens et al., 2018], reporting of incidents on paper and through third parties [Alpert and Macdonald, 2001; Ba et al., 2021], force diversity and peer effects [Ba et al., 2021], and use of past allegations [Rozema and Schanzenbach, 2019]), and new judicial structure (e.g., increased district attorney independence from law enforcement; see Stashko and Garro, 2021).

Cunningham underscored that there has never been a time in the United States when Black people have not been the primary target of state-sanctioned violence. Current use of lethal force is driven primarily by governmental and departmental decisions rather than by "intractable" structural factors; thus, he emphasized that institutions matter and expressed optimism that the public's perception has begun to shift—political reform now seems feasible. He cautioned researchers against focusing too much on new research designs and losing sight of their research questions; context is important when thinking about the best way to answer these questions. In closing, he indicated that quasi-experimental approaches are valuable in that they allow for estimates of causal parameters that policy makers can understand; however, they are weak in that many factors have to align that lie outside of the researchers' control (e.g., data availability, data structure, discontinuities).

QUANTITATIVE HISTORICAL DATA

Amy Kate Bailey (associate professor in the Department of Sociology at the University of Illinois Chicago) discussed the value of incorporating quantitative historical data in models of contemporary health inequities. She explained that because "remnants of the past persist" in people's bodies and in communities, past experiences help to explain current disparities. For example, the social determinants of health paradigm includes specific features of the built environment and the local community, which are fundamentally influenced by historical processes, and life-course and longitudinal approaches embrace links between the past and the present. Furthermore, epigenetic evidence demonstrates that human bodies determine which genes to express based on individual life circumstances and experiences, and genetic inheritances can be passed to future generations. The persistence of culture and inherited trauma also connect directly to historical measures, and biobehavioral responses demonstrate how historical patterns affect current outcomes.

Bailey described her current collaborative research endeavor, which investigates how local histories of racial violence relate to contemporary pregnancy outcomes (e.g., racial inequities in preterm births, low birth weight, and infant mortality). She noted that racial disparities in pregnancy outcomes can first be recognized on a spatial/community level. For example, Black women living in areas of racial isolation have worse pregnancy outcomes than other women (Kramer et al., 2010), and Black infant mortality profiles in states with expanded Medicaid eligibility were better than those in states that did not expand Medicaid eligibility (Bhatt and Beck-Sague, 2018). Additionally, racial economic inequality (Howell et al., 2016; Kothari et al., 2016; Ncube et al., 2016; Siddiqi et al., 2016), local racial climate (Chae et al., 2018; Orchard and Price, 2017), and the 2016 election and immigration raids (Gemmill et al., 2019; Novak, Geronimus, and Martinez-Cardoso, 2017) help to explain racial disparities in pregnancy outcomes. Racial disparities in pregnancy outcomes can also be recognized on an individual level, she continued. For instance, personal experiences with racism, such as living in a racist community, can increase the likelihood of adverse pregnancy outcomes (Bower et al., 2018).

Bailey explained that these current "patterns of injustice" that affect pregnancy outcomes connect directly to historical racial violence. Local histories of racial violence include activities of the Ku Klux Klan in the 1950s (Cunningham and Phillips, 2007; Owens et al., 2015), burnings of Black churches in the late 20th century (McAdam et al., 2013), the development of Southern "segregationist academies" (Porter et al., 2014), hate crimes reporting (King et al., 2009), Black prison admissions (Jacobs et al., 2012), use of the death penalty (Jacobs et al., 2005), White-on-Black homicide (Messner et al., 2005), and corporal punishment in public schools (Ward et al., 2021). She emphasized that enslavement in 1860 is specifically linked both to contemporary conservative political attitudes (Acharya et al., 2016) that affect policy and to racial economic disparities (O'Connell, 2012).

Thus, Bailey asserted that because history and historical contexts operate as a fundamental cause of disease (Figure 2-3), including historical indicators in analyses is essential.

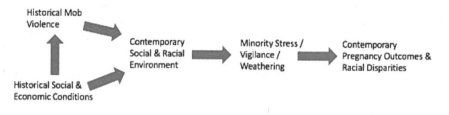

FIGURE 2-3 Tracing the path of history to contemporary health outcomes.
SOURCE: Workshop presentation by Amy Kate Bailey, May 16, 2022.

She underscored that much of the quantitative historical data needed to conduct such analyses already exist—for example, Census data (aggregated data at the state and county levels, and individual data), elections data for state and national offices (down to the county level), Census data of religious bodies, data on legal executions (dating back to the colonial era), data to enable spatial linkages, measures based on vital statistics (aggregated and individual), school enrollment data, and limited administrative record linkages for individuals across the life course. However, she described several challenges in using these data, including an uneven availability of data over space and time, owing to the slow uptake of vital record-keeping across the United States; shifting administrative boundaries that make it difficult to link contemporary measures to the historical context; gaps in historical records that are not randomly distributed (e.g., Census undercounts of marginalized groups); and difficulty in locating and gaining rights to use certain historical data. Bailey highlighted four ways to address these challenges as new historical data continue to be gathered:

1. Additional spatial tools to connect data across time periods and identify spatial relationships within local communities (below the county level);
2. Expanded sources of administratively linked multigenerational records;
3. Better data on local, regional, statewide, and national policies with a focus on their racialized and gendered implications; and
4. Better measures of civil society (e.g., configurations of local business communities).

Bailey emphasized that historical data at both the spatial/community and individual levels have the potential to advance research in health and social equity. For example, she explained that historical data could be used to improve environmental equity. Health researchers already leverage data on historical environmental contaminants and locations of toxic releases but could incorporate additional data from environmental disasters, epidemics, and disease outbreaks to better understand how exposures vary by community. Record linkages then enable the mapping of residential trajectories and related environmental exposures across the life course, including multigenerational exposures and effects. Historical data could also be used to study how inequality and access to opportunity structures affect social and health disparities. Public policies that shaped access to certain resources, the structure of the local labor market, and local school funding could all be analyzed; furthermore, data on multigenerational program participation (e.g., GI bill benefits were mostly for White men) and occupational trajectories could reveal key insights. Lastly, historical data on the social environment could improve understanding of structural racism—for example, data on civil society organizations that supported White supremacy could affect the context of race, gender, and social class; data on voter behavior and suppression could illuminate political power structures; and data on health care structures (e.g., segregated hospitals) could provide insight into local social dynamics. Vital statistics could also be studied to better understand gender relations and women's access to power, both of which are critical to child development and survival.

Bailey identified several challenges with expanded access to such historical data. She cautioned researchers about record "survivability"; not everything recorded survived, and not everything of interest was recorded. Researchers would also benefit from considering the power dynamics associated with what was recorded, by whom, and for what purpose, she continued. Knowing what data are available and gaining permission to access them can be difficult, and tradeoffs between time/labor inputs and accuracy are unavoidable. She described current initiatives to strengthen the use of quantitative historical data, including efforts to digitize historical records, prepare digitized records for quantitative analyses, and make existing records more widely available. For example, the Library of Congress, Zooniverse, the Mellon Foundation, and Humanities without Walls are all engaged in efforts to expand digital access to historical data.

Bailey reiterated that communities and individuals are shaped by their past and that of their ancestors; therefore, researchers could use multiple methodological approaches and forms of data to identify the root causes of social and health inequities. She stressed that accounting for contemporary structural racism without considering the historical legacy that created it is an impossible task.

DATA FOR UNDERSTUDIED POPULATIONS

Desi Small-Rodriguez (assistant professor of sociology and American Indian studies at the University of California, Los Angeles) explained that many populations—at times demographically categorized as "something else"—remain understudied. These populations are often described as difficult to reach and count, hidden, vulnerable, underrepresented, and underserved. However, she emphasized the value of changing these perspectives on understudied populations and the way that they are researched. She asserted that understudied populations are not hidden; rather, they have been historically marginalized, under-resourced, systematically excluded, and deliberately erased. For example, the contemporary racial/ethnic category "American Indian" is a colonizer's term used to identify Indigenous peoples; however, a panethnic American Indian identity did not exist in the precolonial era (Snipp, 1989). Such "colonial myths" persist as mechanisms of Indigenous erasure, she continued, and the intentional effort to erase Indigenous lands and people extends into the data, obscuring inequalities in health care, housing, and education.

Small-Rodriguez stated that researchers and policy makers are limited in their understanding of Indigenous peoples by population definitions that serve the needs of the nation, not the needs of Indigenous communities. For example, government agencies are guided by the following federal definition of American Indian or Alaska Native (AIAN): "a person having origins in any of the original peoples of North and South America (including Central America) and who maintains tribal affiliation or community attachment" (Office of Management and Budget, 1997). According to the 2020 Census, approximately 9.2 million people in the United States identified as AIAN; however, Small-Rodriguez noted that no documented national life expectancy existed for AIAN until 2021, owing to widespread data erasure. Furthermore, at only 71.8 years, this life expectancy is the lowest of any racial/ethnic group—compared with 81.9 years for Hispanic people, 78.8 years for White people, and 74.8 years for Black people (Arias et al, 2021).

Small-Rodriguez suggested that focusing on "peoples" instead of on "populations" would enable movement beyond this type of data erasure. The definition of Indigenous peoplehood—"interlocking concepts of sacred history, ceremonial cycles, language, and ancestral homelands" (Corntassel, 2003)—extends beyond a simple racial category. People data, then, refers to the sovereign nations, which include 574 federally recognized tribes, 326 reservations, and 56 million acres of trust land. To illustrate the complexity of the contemporary Indigenous experience, she explained that blood has become a "sociopolitical and pseudobiological construct of collective identity," and "racial logics continue to distort kinship systems" (see Rodriguez-Lonebear, 2021). She reiterated that the way in which Indigenous peoples have been racialized and erased by federal systems affects data availability and data dependency, and this "assimilative effort to erase" occurs through this "mechanism of blood."

Small-Rodriguez observed that determining who counts as AIAN is further complicated by several different boundaries within the population (Liebler, 2018). For instance, the U.S. Census data exclude one-third of the population of the Northern Cheyenne Nation. Indigenous peoples are thus working to change this narrative of data erasure, stressing both that they are still here and that they are data experts. She emphasized that Indigenous peoples consider data as sacred to sovereignty, and without sovereignty, equity and justice cannot be realized. Indigenous data sovereignty is "the right of Indigenous peoples and nations to govern the collection, ownership, and application of their own data."[1] Indigenous peoples have thus begun to reclaim data sovereignty by decolonizing data, moving from data dependency to control of data by Indigenous peoples and for Indigenous people in all aspects, including collection, analysis, reporting, and storage.

MACHINE LEARNING

Ziad Obermeyer (Blue Cross of California distinguished associate professor of health policy and management at the University of California, Berkeley, School of Public Health) highlighted the danger of algorithms that reproduce and scale up bias in health care, criminal justice, finance, and education. However, some of these dangers can be minimized, he explained, and algorithms could play an important role in fighting bias. To demonstrate the potential for effective algorithm use in the health care space, Obermeyer presented recent research conducted with his colleagues (Pierson et al., 2021) on leveraging algorithms to reduce unexplained pain disparities in underserved populations.

Obermeyer indicated that pain is distributed unequally throughout society and concentrated in the most disadvantaged people—survey evidence reveals that non-White patients experience approximately twice the amount of pain as White patients. In their research, Pierson and colleagues (2021) focused specifically on disparities in knee pain. They noted that the cause for these disparities is far more complex than Black people simply having a higher incidence of osteoarthritis in the knee—Black, lower-income, and lower-education patients reported more knee pain, despite the similarity in the degree of osteoarthritis revealed in the X-rays of their knees and those of White patients. This raised an important question: if the knee is not causing the pain, what is?

Reflecting on various possible explanations for this pain gap from existing scholarship, Obermeyer stated that when experiencing similar stimuli, people with higher levels of stress often have more pain than people with

---

[1] See https://nni.arizona.edu/programs-projects/policy-analysis-research/indigenous-data-sovereignty-and-governance

lower levels of stress. For example, anxiety and depression can manifest as pain, and, in some communities, demands for attention toward other aspects of life might decrease one's ability to cope with pain. Furthermore, he noted that the medical system provides less access to pain management therapies for some communities than for others.

Obermeyer described the typical process used to address pain: a patient describes his or her pain to a doctor, who then orders an X-ray. The doctor reviews the X-ray's appearance and "grades" it to determine disease severity based on certain criteria, most of which were developed in 1957. These grading scales were developed on one population, homogeneous in race and sex, and may not generalize to the populations seeking care today, Obermeyer asserted. As a result, when human radiologists determine that a knee is not diseased, they might overlook the real causes of knee pain in disadvantaged groups. Although measuring disease severity might seem like the perfect task for an algorithm, he continued, algorithms are usually trained to match human performance (i.e., the radiologist's review of the X-ray for disease severity), which is not the desired outcome in this case, because something would still be missing.

Therefore, Obermeyer advocated for the algorithm to be trained differently—to listen to the patient (instead of learning from the radiologist) and predict the degree of pain that will be reported based on a given X-ray. He mentioned that data that link X-rays to radiologists' interpretations are abundant, but data on the link between X-rays and patient pain experience are much sparser. However, once such data are available, measuring disease severity could become a straightforward machine-learning problem. Thus, an algorithm could help confirm that if the pain is predictable from the X-ray of the knee, the pain is coming from the knee, and if it is not, other causes could be explored. Pierson and colleagues (2021) found that the algorithm explains nearly half of the pain gap between Black and White patients, which is far more than what radiologists account for in their interpretations. Obermeyer pointed out that decision-making currently depends on radiologists' perspectives. Guidelines for receiving a life-transforming knee replacement, for example, are based on both the severity of knee pain and the severity of knee disease; by inserting the algorithm's prediction of severity to make this decision instead of relying on the radiologist's assessment, the fraction of Black people eligible for knee replacement doubled.

Obermeyer underscored that algorithms have the potential to perform better than humans instead of reproducing their errors and biases. To achieve this, he continued, algorithms in the field of medicine should learn from nature (i.e., patient experiences and health outcomes). However, because data on patient outcomes and experiences are siloed, and the infrastructure to connect good researchers with good data does not currently exist, researchers are working toward a solution to move the field forward. For example, Nightingale Open Science[2] works with health systems, companies, and governments to build data infrastructure and curate datasets around unsolved medical problems, with a focus on high-priority problems and populations—these deidentified datasets are then accessible to nonprofit researchers on a cloud platform for free.

REFLECTIONS AND DISCUSSION

Serving as the first discussant for this session, Takeuchi commended the speakers for their efforts to include new designs, methods, and populations in the study of structural racism, and expressed his support for the development of theories for structural racism that align with methods to best uncover drivers of health outcomes. He cautioned that without such theoretical frameworks, structural racism research could become a cottage industry.

Reflecting on recent research endeavors, Takeuchi noted that of all of the projects funded by the National Institutes of Health between 2018 and 2022, 41,784 focused on health disparities. However, less than two percent of those projects mentioned racism, and only about 25 projects included a theory of racism. Less than 20 of these projects used historical, machine learning, or experimental approaches, suggesting that these methods are significantly underused in the study of systemic racism and health. Furthermore, Takeuchi reported, only a small number of the funded projects on racism focused on Indigenous peoples, Asian Americans, Native Hawaiians, and Pacific Islanders. He also reflected specifically on an article published in 1970 that said that Black, Indigenous, and other people of color were less likely than White people to seek care for mental health issues, and when they did, they received lower-quality care and experienced poor health outcomes. Despite significant improvements in mental health care and increases in the number of people insured, the same pattern of findings persists in 2022. He asserted that combining new theories and new methods with conventional approaches could begin to address these issues more systematically.

Opening the general discussion, Frank Edwards (assistant professor of criminal justice at Rutgers University) expressed his interest in learning more about the gap between Census data and tribal data described by Small-Rodriguez. He wondered if the source of the bias has been decomposed (i.e., who was missing from the Census data but captured in the tribal data?) and how contemporary data could be used alongside historical data to understand event exposure and population change over time. Small-Rodriguez suggested the need for increased linkages between tribal data

---

[2] See www.nightingalescience.org

and other existing data, and she encouraged demographers and researchers to support this work, with tribes in control and tribal leaders cogoverning the process. For example, uncovering why younger populations from the Northern Cheyenne population were overrepresented in the Census data as compared with the tribal data is important. She noted that tribal nations are acutely aware that they are undercounted in the Census, which underscores the need to continue to leverage the data that tribes are collecting. Seth Sanders (Ronald Ehrenberg professor of economics at Cornell University) agreed that the tribes are in the best position to generate the data of most interest to their communities. At the same time, he continued, because comparative work is important for science, parallel data collected outside of the tribes would be useful to address certain questions. He considered the use of panel data for this purpose but wondered who would have access to those data. He advocated for the use of models that simultaneously benefit science, give control to sovereign nations, and help to develop the human capital of tribes. Small-Rodriguez emphasized the value of creating a tribal data standard in the United States, which would enable increased opportunities with comparative data. Furthermore, she pointed out that the United States has never conducted a national survey of Indigenous peoples, unlike its peer countries.

Reflecting on the Latin American experience in particular, Flores remarked that the process of defining who is Indigenous is complicated, which has implications for measures of inequality. He asked about the gold standard for the measurement of inequality in Native American populations in the United States. Small-Rodriguez explained that identifying a gold standard is not feasible since each tribe is its own nation, and the heterogeneity within a tribal population can be even greater than that between populations. She said that a community partnership would be beneficial to study the comparisons within and between tribes.

A participant pointed out that community-engaged primary data collection can be costly and time consuming but wondered whether using secondary data, which are easier to access but lack context, removes a researcher too much from the communities of interest. Flores explained that he first develops a research question, collects primary data through several methods (e.g., focus groups and personal interviews), and designs his own experiments, but he uses secondary data to corroborate his observations. Cunningham said that his work relies on secondary data, but he also makes an effort to talk to police officers to engage different perspectives: their opinions might reveal different takeaways that could be placed in historical context. Bailey commented that her work is almost exclusively in the analysis of secondary data, but she personally builds many of those datasets from historical archival data. She suggested collaborating with students, if they are available, to build these datasets as well as to embed contemporary outcomes within a historical context to help avoid disengagement. Obermeyer added that his inspiration comes from clinical work, including difficult decision-making about patient care in the emergency room. However, that level of engagement does not have to come from direct practice; ethical research includes talking to people and investing time to amass information about institutions to identify quasi-experimental variation. A self-described "data rebuilder," Small-Rodriguez said that she uses secondary data and identifies opportunities to creatively link existing data for populations that remain understudied. She emphasized that secondary research does indeed help to support community needs.

A participant posed a question about whether the term stereotype has only negative connotations. Flores responded that stereotypes are complex because they are explanations that one group provides about another; they could be positive, negative, or ambiguous. For example, being "stubborn" could be either positive or negative, because the meaning of a stereotype is based on a particular social context. However, he pointed out that some of the methodologies used for stereotype research are not yet designed to capture meaning.

Trevon Logan (workshop planning committee member and Hazel C. Youngberg distinguished professor of economics at The Ohio State University) added that stereotypes about White people have to be "positive," owing to the structure of racialization, and researchers have a responsibility to interrogate this language. He also highlighted the importance of key language distinctions related to structural racism; for example, mistrust is based on intuition, and distrust is based on experiences. He stressed the value of choosing words carefully when engaging in structural racism research—for example, distrust better frames conversations about Native populations' feelings toward the dominant population than mistrust. Reflecting on the connection between language and the use of algorithmic approaches to understand pain experiences and socioeconomic outcomes, he observed that interrogating science while using the language of science is difficult for inherently racialized processes.

A participant wondered whether the U.S. Food and Drug Administration could play a regulatory role in ensuring that algorithms eliminate rather than replicate biases. Obermeyer highlighted his work auditing algorithms that are widely used in the health care space and finding a significant amount of racial bias (e.g., algorithms that deprioritize care for sicker Black patients in favor of healthier White patients). He described this as a significant market failure, in that this bias could have been caught before the software was implemented. Thus, he championed the role of regulation; the next step is to determine what to regulate. He mentioned that drug regulation offers a useful precedent for algorithm regulation: one first defines the outcome before obtaining drug approval. Similarly, determining the information that the algorithm should produce would create the standard by which the algorithm would be held accountable for biases and for accuracy (see Bembeneck et al., 2021). Lee inquired about the potential for machine learning or other approaches to capture more informal processes by which people's needs are not being addressed—for example, pain patients who are not approved to have magnetic resonance imaging (MRI) and so are not included in the training dataset for the algorithm. Obermeyer responded that an anterior cruciate ligament tear, for example, can only be observed in an MRI; thus, prediction is based on those who have access to an MRI—that is, the algorithm can predict a biological event but only conditional on having the MRI. He cautioned against the practice of infusing disparities to access into the algorithms and emphasized that steps can be taken so that the algorithm can generalize to people who have not had the MRI. He encouraged a careful, detective-like approach to addressing disparities that surface in datasets, which could lead to improving the performance of algorithms for health care and redistributing resources to patients in need. In some settings, however, such as criminal justice, he asserted that no such workarounds exist because the data are too biased, and algorithms might not be the best approach.

MIXED METHODS APPROACHES

Paris "AJ" Adkins-Jackson (assistant professor in the departments of Epidemiology and Sociomedical Sciences in the Mailman School of Public Health at Columbia University) explained that racism assigns value and discriminates (Jones, 2000), and that racism has multiple levels—for example, interpersonal, internalized, institutional, intraorganizational, and extraorganizational (Griffith et al., 2007; Jones et al., 2019)—and multiple dimensions—for example, via residential segregation, access to health care, and civics (Bailey et al., 2017). Structural racism, she continued, occurs across the life course, influencing educational, social, and economic opportunities, as well as leading to immediate (e.g., injury) and cumulative (e.g., multimorbidity) health effects (Glymour and Manly, 2008).

Adkins-Jackson presented strategies for combatting structural racism using mixed methods. She encouraged researchers to pair methodological tools, such as surveys, observations, biomarkers, ethnologies, social media, interviews, photovoice, archives, and ethnographies, to better understand the complexity of structural racism. The use of mixed methods can be done sequentially (i.e., quantitative before qualitative) or concurrently (i.e., qualitative plus quantitative) to explicate a phenomenon about which there is limited information, to corroborate existing evidence, or to dispute existing evidence. Mixed methods designs can be correlational/causal, experimental, phenomenological, or comparative, or can take the form of case study or grounded theory (Johnson et al., 2007). She described case studies and comparative analyses as particularly effective approaches to leverage multiple methods for the study of structural racism.

Adkins-Jackson offered two examples of recent effective mixed methods research. First, she highlighted the work of Ashley Gripper (Drexel University), who used grounded theory and the sequential mixed methods of an interview followed by a survey—which is a common approach in the field of psychology—to explicate the experiences of urban farmers and their understanding of environmental justice and health. Second, she described the work of Brittney Butler (Harvard University), who created a comparative study using the concurrent mixed methods approach of collecting survey data, observation data, and interview data to corroborate the impact of anti-Black racism on birthing individuals across different datasets.

Adkins-Jackson cautioned researchers against becoming nonreflexive scientists, who are unaware of how much harm they create by preselecting methods—a decision that immediately introduces bias into a study. To avoid introducing bias, she encouraged researchers to recognize that structural racism is experienced by people; it is not merely a scientific exploration. She also stressed that structural racism researchers take care to avoid practicing racism themselves: both collaborators' and participants' contributions to the research have value. Thus, true reflexive scientists practice self-reflexivity (Ford and Arhihenbuwa, 2010; Hardeman and Karbeah, 2020), partner with the community (Leung et al., 2004), read and cite scholars from historically marginalized communities (Onwuegbuzie and Collins, 2007), collaborate with interdisciplinary colleagues, and examine methodological frameworks.

Emphasizing the value of theoretical and methodological frameworks in particular, Adkins-Jackson explained that a theory shapes the relationship between an exposure and an outcome (e.g., critical race theory, intersectionality [Crenshaw et al., 1996], and fundamental cause theory [Phelan and Link, 2013, 2015]). A methodological framework, then, guides the methods and analyses based on the existing research question. Reflecting on the concepts that support perspectives about phenomena, she observed that many people have a positivist perspective—that is, a fixed, objective reality that can be understood through logic and reasoning. However, she posited that if knowledge is cocreated, multiple truths will arise with no fixed destination; therefore, a social constructivist perspective facilitates an understanding of the meaning derived from these multiple truths, as well as a particular phenomenon's impact on a community, which is the desired measurement in structural racism research.

As an example of using mixed methods to examine the impact of structural racism on a community, she described the work of the late Candice Rice (University of California, San Diego). Rice used concurrently observation, archives, and autoethnography, as well as a case study on the impact on Black mothers of crime and substance abuse policies enacted after the 1992 Los Angeles uprising, to dispute the idea that poor behaviors create these policies; rather, these policies lead to poor behaviors. Furthermore, the data from this and other mixed methods research revealed that high stress leads to poor health for Black women in particular (see also Adkins-Jackson et al., 2019). The women's specific narratives illuminated a form of structural gendered racism, pointing to the White supremacist, patriarchal, heteronormative, able-centric system as a cause of poor health for Black women: a system that impacts the larger Black communities for which "Black women are socialized to care" (see Adkins-Jackson et al., 2022; Laster Pirtle and Wright, 2021).

PLACE-BASED APPROACHES

Michelle Johnson-Jennings (professor at the University of Washington and director of the Environmentally-based Health & Land-based Healing Division at the Indigenous Wellness Research Institute) described an Indigenous perspective on place, and she depicted the use of Indigenous land-based healing to improve community health and well-being and to combat structural racism.

Johnson-Jennings remarked that for the Choctaw people in particular, land is central to health and well-being. In order to illuminate this Indigenous connection to place, she compared the health frameworks of Indigenous peoples with those of people who practice Western medicine. The Indigenous framework for health and healing outlines that the ancestors provide instructions for interacting with the land and offer gifts of strength and health; relationships with nature are important to preserving health, and illness arises from an imbalance in these relationships; and healing is space-, place-, and community-oriented. In essence, she continued, Indigenous people believe that they can be healthy only if their land is healthy. This framework contrasts that of Western health, in which ancestors pass on their diseases to the next generation; mind, body, spirit, and nature are disconnected; illness arises from microagents; and land has no place or relationship in healing.

Acknowledging the presence of Indigenous peoples, Johnson-Jennings explained, demands recognition of the objectification, enslavement, marginalization, oppression, and genocide they have experienced. The erasure of "the problem of Indigenous people" has been both systematic and purposeful: historical attacks (e.g., massacres, warfare, illegal sterilization), removals (e.g., illegal healing practices, starvation, land allotment), and assimilation policies (e.g., boarding schools, nutrition experiments, and animal husbandry) are reflected in the structural racism experienced by Indigenous communities today through limited access to health care, self-determination restrictions, and environmental pollutants on reservations. She provided several examples of these systematic methods to eradicate Indigenous place and being, including body objectification in the 17th and 18th centuries; a movement toward eugenics with feeblemindedness starting in the 19th century; and the development of IQ tests with Indigenous people as the deficit to justify both their removal and their sterilization (see, e.g., Fitzgerald and Ludeman, 1926; Garth, 1931). According to Johnson-Jennings, 25–50 percent of all AIAN children were removed from their homes and placed in foster care or boarding schools in the 1940s, and at least 25 percent of Native women of childbearing age across the United States were sterilized by 1976 (see Lawrence, 2000).

Johnson-Jennings indicated that these systematic, place-based attacks on Indigenous people continued throughout the 20th century. By either removing Indigenous people from their sacred land or confining them to certain places, the culture continued to be erased. *Place* for Indigenous people thus became defined by vulnerability, discrimination, and a lack of control, and she asserted that these colonial narratives of the past continue to have negative impacts on Native people (e.g., gaps in educational opportunities and issues with law enforcement). The historical trauma of this structural racism within Indigenous communities can be understood as the "cumulative emotional and psychological wounding over the lifespan and across generations, emanating from massive group trauma experiences" (see Brave Heart, 1998, 1999, 2003).

Johnson-Jennings underscored that although Indigenous people are working to recover from this historical trauma, it compounds present trauma in the form of increased risk of disease susceptibility. She stressed that this context is particularly important for researchers who want to better understand Indigenous health issues. For example, racial discrimination can increase pain and can lead to increased rates of smoking among individuals in the AIAN community (Johnson-Jennings et al., 2014). However, despite this history of suffering, she emphasized that Indigenous communities are resilient. This trauma can be transformed by fostering supportive relationships and engaging in the traditional Indigenous land-based practices for innovative healing—that is, "(re)connecting to the land and centering the land in order to conduct healing, or a health intervention" (Johnson-Jennings et al., 2020).

Johnson-Jennings also accentuated the value of decolonizing research by recovering subjugated knowledges and documenting social injustice. Doing so creates a voice for the silenced and challenges racism, colonialism, and oppression (Smith, 2021). Most importantly, this decolonizing of health research helps to create a place where Indigenous peoples can survive and thrive, "guided by their ancestral knowledges and practices centered upon the lands" (see Johnson-Jennings et al., 2019, 2020).

NOVEL APPROACHES TO SURVEY DATA

Courtney Boen (assistant professor of sociology at the University of Pennsylvania) provided an overview of how longitudinal social surveys can be used to explore the structural, institutional, and relational processes that produce and maintain racialized inequities in health and other outcomes, with particular attention to how better data infrastructure and methodological approaches could center equity and justice. She noted that these types of surveys (e.g., the National Longitudinal Study of Adolescent to Adult Health; National Social Life, Health, and Aging Project; Fragile Families and Child Wellbeing Study) engage a life-course perspective, which considers health and aging as lifelong processes, incorporates the timing and duration of exposures, evaluates how the past shapes the future, and links lives to better illuminate the emergence of inequities across the life span.

Boen pointed out, however, that the use of social surveys to explore racialized inequities is not without theoretical, epistemological, and methodological challenges. First, race is typically operationalized in survey research as a static, individual-level trait rather than understood as a proxy for complex, dynamic, relational processes of historical and contemporary racialization and racism. Reflecting on the ideas of sociologist Tukufu Zuberi, she explained that racial categories continue to be used to justify structural racism and White supremacy, but much survey research still includes a variable for race without consideration for what that measure represents. Second, she observed that survey research often promotes methodological individualism, which emphasizes the study of individuals or groups who experience oppression and discrimination rather than the study of the racist systems that oppress, discriminate, and create inequities. Third, although conventional regression estimators are a key aspect of survey research, they can be misaligned with relational theories of race and racism.

Boen remarked that the first step in improving the use of survey research to understand the drivers of racialized health inequities is to have better data to capture the structural and institutional processes that produce these inequities, as well as better data infrastructure. She encouraged researchers to recognize that individual-level measures are imperfect and imprecise proxies for complex systems of social relations (e.g., *race* as a function of historical and contemporary processes of racialization and racism; and *socioeconomic status* as the product of exploitation, theft, and extraction). This awareness can shift the research focus from the individuals who experience harm to the systems that create the harm. However, she underscored that such a shift also demands data linkages to illuminate those processes that maintain structural racism. These data linkages could be enabled with increased funding and publishing incentives to share policy, institutional, and contextual data as well as increased priorities to reduce administrative barriers. For example, Boen described current research that links county-level data on Immigration and Customs Enforcement with state immigration policy data and geocoded Health and Retirement Study data to better understand how changes in county-level immigration enforcement and state law affect individual- and group-level changes in health risk across adulthood (Boen et al., forthcoming). Legal violence against immigrants, Boen and colleagues argue, has implications for the production of racialized inequities in health: increases in county-level immigration enforcement led to increased health risks among foreign-born Hispanic adults in particular. In a related study, state-level immigration policy data were linked to data from the National Agricultural Workers Survey and revealed that restrictive state-level immigration policies shape racialized legal status inequities and health care use among U.S. agricultural workers. Non-White workers experienced the most significant barriers to health care (e.g., high cost, lack of information, lack of access to transportation, fear of legal status being discovered) after these policies were implemented (Schut and Boen, forthcoming). Boen summarized that both studies highlight how data linkages can be used effectively to explore the institutional drivers of population health gaps.

Boen discussed another common approach used to measure structural racism that focuses solely on markers of disparities and discrimination in particular institutional domains, which can conceal other forms and consequences of racial violence, racist social control, and structural racism. Thus, she encouraged researchers to also consider how overall levels of exploitation, violence, exclusion, and social control can reflect the structural racism that affects social inequities. Several systems (e.g., legal, health care, and welfare) emerging from historical and contemporary racism attempt to maintain the racial order; Boen asserted that researchers' methods to measure structural racism should reflect this reality.

Boen explained that a second step in improving the use of survey research for understanding the drivers of racialized inequities is to develop methods that better align with critical, dynamic, and relational theories of race and racism. She noted that social survey research relies heavily on conventional regression estimators and focuses on identifying the causal effect of discrimination; however, this approach is limited. A question arises about the possibility of separating "nonrace" variables from "race" (i.e., proxies for processes of racialization and structural and institutional racism)—a separation she portrayed as untenable. This challenge is compounded with longitudinal data, for which conventional regression assumes an absence of time-varying relationships among the variables that is inconsistent with dynamic theories of race and racialization. In an attempt to overcome the limitations of conventional regression in identifying the life-course social exposures of racialized inequities, Graetz and colleagues (2022) suggest that the parametric G-formula be used to better theorize and model mediators as connected to a system of historical and contemporary racism and racialization—that is, instead of separating variables by "nonrace" and "race," everything is treated as a mediator (see also Aislinn Bohren et al., 2022).

In closing, Boen remarked that identifying the dynamic processes that enable the production of racialized inequities in health and other outcomes across the life course and across generations has the potential to advance science, intervention, and policy; social surveys are well-suited for this work but only if the data and methods match the theory. She asserted that data and methods that ignore structural and institutional processes that generate inequities are insufficient, and better data linkages and expansion beyond approaches that separate "race" from "nonrace" are critical. She emphasized that causal inference research using survey data does not have to be used to identify marginal effects that inform well-defined interventions (Schwartz et al., 2016). The next step, she continued, is to incorporate methods for modeling the historical and dynamic life-course processes that maintain racist social systems and to build data infrastructure that captures the complex processes that create health inequities; these actions could support more holistic ideas about how racialized inequities in health and other outcomes have been produced and move society closer to achieving equity and justice.

NOVEL APPROACHES TO
ADMINISTRATIVE AND CROWD-SOURCED DATA

Frank Edwards (assistant professor of criminal justice at Rutgers University) described his interest in using descriptive methods and novel data to quantify the social distribution of state violence in both historical and contemporary ways. He explained that novel data not only present new opportunities to measure state violence but also reveal the limits of official statistics. Currently, although public data on the activities of violent U.S. state institutions for the purposes of research and evaluation are often sparse and of low quality because they rely on self-reporting by law enforcement agencies, internal data holdings for the purposes of surveillance and control are significant. He stressed, however, that this data opacity is a feature rather than a flaw of public systems that administer state violence. For example, states collect information to enhance their operations; state agencies that engage in violence collect data to target people and increase power. He cautioned researchers to be mindful of these types of data-generating processes.

Edwards emphasized that no official source of data on police violence in the United States exists. He described Fatal Encounters—an unofficial source of data on police violence collected by a single journalist—which uses searchable news archives to create a streaming dataset that captures all deaths occurring during contact with law enforcement prior to entrance into a correctional institution. These data reveal that 3.2 people were killed per day by police use of force in the United States between 2013 and 2021. The National Vital Statistics System from the Centers for Disease Control and Prevention, however, reported only 1.6 people killed per day during the same time frame (Figure 2-4). Edwards explained that this discrepancy highlights an issue in the data-generating process: underreporting. For instance, if the cause of death was not labeled by the medical examiner as "by law enforcement," it is not recorded as such.

Edwards noted that this example demonstrates the value of un-official data sources; however, he encouraged researchers to use novel data cautiously and critically, as unofficial data are not without challenges and biases. For instance, searchable local news data could have temporal biases, especially given that online news was not fully accessible across the nation until 2010. As a second example of the use of novel data, Edwards described research with colleague Sadaf Hashimi on the age-specific risk of police use of force in New Jersey. The data from legally mandated force reports collected by a local news organization, NJ Direct, appear to

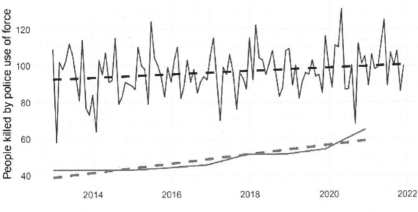

Fatal encounters (black); NVSS (red) with linear trend (dashed)

Average daily killings – FE: 3.2 ; NVSS: 1.6
Average monthly killings – FE: 96.5 ; NVSS: 49.8
Average yearly killings – FE: 1157.7 ; NVSS: 597

data from fatalencounters.org and CDC

FIGURE 2-4 Number of people killed by police use of force as reported by Fatal Encounters (black line) and by the National Vital Statistics System (red line), with linear trend (dashed lines).
SOURCE: Workshop presentation by Frank Edwards, May 17, 2022.

show high levels of force against young Black men; however, the data are incomplete because the levels of reporting compliance vary significantly across New Jersey, likely owing to variation in policy and training across the state's 450 police departments. Thus, he explained that because under-reporting leads to missing data, these estimates are likely undercounts and would be considered lower bounds.

Edwards mentioned that administrative data, another type of novel data, are generated routinely for the administration of various state programs and collected to meet organizational needs and for legal compliance; they are not produced with the research community in mind. Looking at administrative data on prenatal substance exposure screening from 2010 through 2019 from the National Child Abuse and Neglect Data System, Edwards and his colleagues found that in Minnesota, for example, American Indian infants were 15 times more likely than White infants to be reported to child protection agencies with infant or prenatal substance exposure. This type of study of administrative data is important, he continued, but despite federal requirements to collect them, these data are missing from at least 20 states. He reiterated that researchers should interpret the data with a critical eye amid issues of nonreporting and spatial bias.

Reflecting on the future, Edwards emphasized that official data collection is likely not the best path forward owing to federalism and the diffusion of oversight (i.e., with more than 10,000 law enforcement agencies in the United States, much data reporting is voluntary), as well as to issues of historical and contemporary racial politics and data asymmetry. He underscored the value of building infrastructure for unofficial data collection, especially to track state violence. He added that because news data are powerful but limited, funders and universities could commit to long-term streaming data collection, which is relatively inexpensive yet invaluable. Administrative data on state violence in particular have several challenges: agency administrative data can be of high quality but are often limited in scope geographically, and agency involvement in approval processes limits the scope of critical research when researchers are not granted access to datasets. He asserted that new processes for managing data access and linking administrative datasets that would be independent of state agencies and administered more impartially could enable critical research on structural racism.

REFLECTIONS AND DISCUSSION

Serving as the second discussant for this session, Flores observed that all of the speakers highlighted the complexity of the study of structural racism, which has medical, social, educational, psychological, and historical dimensions. The systems of racial oppression—for example, environmental pollution and land impacts, immigration policies, and criminal justice issues—vary across populations. He reiterated that understanding these systems is essential to appreciate how structural racism shapes people's lives. He also reflected on the modeling challenges described by some of the session's speakers and agreed that researchers would benefit from recognizing that race is fluid and shaped by the context and history of a place, with different consequences for different individuals. Since some methods can produce biases, he continued, listening to narratives about people's experiences with discrimination and oppression and using methodologies that incorporate this community knowledge is essential. Flores noted that speakers also stressed the importance of incorporating and linking many types of data to match the complexity of structural racism, although challenges arise here too. For example, because administrative data likely underreport oppression and violence, other sources that complement and interrogate these official sources of data are critical. With all of these complex challenges in mind, he encouraged researchers to reflect on a key question: how can systems of knowledge be created that develop more insight on structural racism?

A participant inquired about barriers to forming interdisciplinary teams for structural racism research, as well as strategies to overcome them. Adkins-Jackson encouraged researchers to think more broadly about using science to achieve justice in the real world. That mindset could lead to the creation of more balanced teams to move forward with collaborative research. Edwards mentioned existing professional barriers to justice-focused work, and he suggested that quantitative researchers would benefit from greater humility and openness toward other paths to knowledge. Johnson-Jennings advocated for the development of research protocols in collaboration with the community of interest, which prioritizes a focus on science for the common good that could impact future generations positively. Boen pointed out that disciplinary norms related to publishing, funding, and career trajectories present challenges for interdisciplinary research; however, the best science happens "on the fringes" and at the intersections of disciplines. She urged researchers to leverage tools from several disciplines to examine complex social problems and to overcome barriers to achieving justice- and equity-oriented science. Another participant wondered about the impacts of these contrasting disciplinary norms, especially when funders assume the role of gatekeepers that give preference to short products that do not have the space to incorporate the voices of communities. Boen replied that although interdisciplinary teams continue to face challenges, funders are now more accepting of the role that these teams play in addressing complex issues such as structural racism. Institutional supports help facilitate these collaborations, she continued, but they can still be difficult, especially when a decision has to be made about where to publish the research. She encouraged researchers to be honest and transparent about expectations for authorship and funding at the start of any collaboration. Adkins-Jackson emphasized the need to move beyond viewing only publications and career trajectories as the end products of collaboration.

A participant inquired about successful examples of incorporating community voices into research. Johnson-Jennings described her experiences working with the Choctaw Nation on land-based healing to address the historical trauma of structural racism and related health disparities. She said that they avoid "wallowing in the trauma and the drama" of the past, and instead study the ancestors' archival narratives with a focus on healing and resilience for future generations. She advocated for grassroots initiatives that center on love from the community and its needs, instead of on the trauma, with community members contributing throughout the process.

Logan asked how researchers could think about data specifically as a tool for narrative. Edwards suggested that researchers observe movements on the ground that are striving for justice and consider how data could be used to support those stories. In other words, he continued, researchers could take different forms of knowledge, translate it into different domains, and search in new ways for known concepts. Johnson-Jennings added that data should be investigated in relation to how they have reinforced structural racism in communities—data reframing and renarration are often crucial for this task. Boen mentioned that although quantitative scholars often focus on complex models of causal inference for validation, great power can be found by linking the descriptive analysis of stories to rich, critical theory.

Another participant asked how best to evaluate the reliability of data collected by private entities. Edwards noted that all data analysis demands strong detective work—that is, thinking carefully and critically about data-generating processes as well as data quality (e.g., using reasonable priors for assessment). Adkins-Jackson championed Cunningham's previously discussed strategy of asking the community of interest and other stakeholders for their opinions on research findings as one effective way to test the validity and reliability of data.

3

Moving Forward: Data Infrastructure Needs in Harnessing Data for Research in Structural Racism

Key Points Highlighted by Presenters

- Power is a fundamental driver of health and equity; collective power and political will are necessary for aligning critical data and research tools in order to improve methods and measurement in structural racism research. (Marjory Givens)
- With greater attention to diversity in the data collection planning process and increased involvement from stakeholders in data-related decision-making, large panel datasets such as the National Longitudinal Study of Youth could be used to study structural racism by providing useful indicators of cumulative disadvantage and revealing how racism moves across institutions. (Seth Sanders)
- A sustainable infrastructure for research on structural racism, health, and aging includes funding for longitudinal design and core support for multiple types of data, multidisciplinary research teams with proven competence and expertise in health equity research, and incentives to focus research frameworks on structural and policy change. (Jennifer Manly)
- A nationally, publicly available data repository for use by researchers, community members, and policy makers will enable a better understanding of how structural racism is operating and its impact on population health and well-being. (Rachel Hardeman)

HARNESSING DATA FOR RESEARCH ON STRUCTURAL RACISM

Marjory Givens (associate director of the University of Wisconsin Population Health Institute and co-director of County Health Rankings & Roadmaps) emphasized that data are needed for measuring and model-

47

ing structural racism, as well as for identifying and measuring the mechanisms that link racism to population health and well-being over time. She described power—which can be visible, hidden, or invisible—as a fundamental driver of health and equity (Lukes, 2005). Influencing the invisible face of power are data and narrative, which reveal "value-based meta-stories" about how the world functions and affect public consciousness (i.e., societal responsibility and possibility).

Givens indicated that many scholars have discussed the value of thinking critically about measurement, as well as about how the power of narrative and data can be used to advance change. She underscored the goal to harness data to "ensure that public infrastructure and social systems nurture collective well-being and help create the conditions where everyone has what they need to thrive." For example, Givens and colleagues (2021) highlight the value of critical race praxis, which asks structural racism researchers to consider their research inquiries and applicable disciplinary knowledge in light of the following question: Who decides what matters and what is measurable? The researchers document the power maintained by those who determine what can be measured, how to invest in data infrastructure, and who can access the data; they note that seemingly objective choices about methodology have important implications both for the research and for future policy.

Reflecting on how existing data could be leveraged to strengthen structural racism research, Givens explained that theory-based methodological approaches offer historical and geographical context and engage both qualitative and quantitative methods that portray the systemic features of structural racism (Hardeman et al., 2022). Such methodological approaches are particularly important within a data system that is structurally racist, she continued. For example, the tax code is only one of many systems that reinforce the racial wealth divide over the life course and across generations—credit scoring, lending, Medicaid expansion, and higher education are others. According to Dorothy Brown (2021), "tax policies ignore the day-to-day reality of most black Americans, who are still playing catch-up in a system that deliberately excluded them for many years." To illustrate the magnitude of this racial wealth divide, Givens pointed out that according to the 2019 Survey of Consumer Finances the median household wealth in the United States in 2019 was $24,100 for Black Americans and $188,200 for White Americans, a disparity that has persisted for decades.

Givens underscored that repeated practices and policies create, contribute to, and maintain this racial wealth divide; as wealth is passed from generation to generation, people are born into different levels of opportunity. Although many U.S. households build wealth through home ownership, Black households are at a disadvantage owing to discriminatory housing and lending practices, for example. Furthermore, community wealth is key to funding public goods and community infrastructure such as schools and parks. In other words, she continued, racism and the racial wealth divide have tangible implications, such as geographic differences in school funding—the most significant deficits are in the Southern Black Belt, a region with a long history of structural racism that continues to affect community resources.

Givens asserted that addressing this structural racism requires both data and political will.

She accentuated that data have been and will continue to be "politicized and weaponized"; for instance, the U.S. Census, which is essential for public health, has been "structurally flawed and racist from [its] origins" (Krieger, 2019) and has been used as a political instrument (e.g., the attempt to exclude unauthorized immigrants from the 2020 Census counts for representation). Therefore, she stated that data to examine the mechanisms that link racism to population health and well-being over time are essential.

Givens also explained that conceptual frameworks can shape "how we make sense of the world: what we measure, how, and why." For example, population health researchers have begun to develop graphic representations of health and its many drivers. Such health and equity frameworks can serve several purposes, such as informing research agendas, serving as boundary-spanning tools for engagement, helping organize thoughts and shape narratives, and raising awareness of the interconnections that affect health and equity. She summarized a review of 27 graphic representations from the population health community published during the 21st century (Givens et al., 2020): few articulated underlying theories; most were found in publicly available grey literature, but only eight were published in peer-reviewed literature; earlier frameworks were intended to guide policy development or research, and more recent frameworks focused on community practice or research; and more than half acknowledged the existence of inequities in determinants or policies, while half mentioned multiple disparity domains. Most did not address how health outcomes or determinants are distributed across populations or the drivers that influence variation in those distributions. Only nine frameworks identified some drivers as "fundamental" or "root" causes of health inequity, and the terminology varied (i.e., only nine explicitly named "racism," and five included political or institutional "power" as drivers of health and equity). Two of the frameworks that explicitly named racism as fundamental or sociocultural drivers were those developed by Schulz and Northridge (2004) and Hill and colleagues (2015). Frameworks that named power as a fundamental driver include those developed by the University of Wisconsin (2019), Public Health Scotland (2016), and ChangeLab Solutions (2019). She explained that the variation across these frameworks suggests that the population health community has not reached consensus on the drivers of health and equity, which has implications for measurement, methods, and understanding of the mechanisms that link racism to population health and well-being over time.

In closing, Givens shared an excerpt from a poem by Ryan Petteway (2022) entitled "Something something something by race, 2021," which offers commentary on the dominant paradigm for the production of racial health inequities: "structural racism [is] not just a thing 'out there' to study in relation to health inequities, but also a thing 'in here' that shapes how we do what we do and who gets to do it." She described this poem as a call to action for researchers. Givens outlined next steps for the population health community to better harness data for structural racism research: (1) use collective power and political will to mobilize the full range of data and research tools; (2) look inward, at history, and toward the future to improve methods and measurement; and (3) align practices and tools more effectively to leverage the power of data and narrative.

A RESEARCH OPPORTUNITY: A NEW COHORT OF THE NATIONAL LONGITUDINAL SURVEY OF YOUTH

Seth Sanders (Ronald Ehrenberg professor of economics at Cornell University) indicated that population representative panel datasets (i.e., data collected by following people over long periods of time) appear to be well-suited to studying the effects of structural racism because they create opportunities for linkages (e.g., criminal justice outcomes to late labor market success) and for the measurement of cumulative effects; however, these studies are not ideal for that purpose. He asserted that a new cohort of the National Longitudinal Survey of Youth (NLSY) could mitigate existing issues and become valuable for structural racism research.

Sanders highlighted six key strengths of national longitudinal surveys in relation to the study of structural racism.

1. Data collection typically begins when respondents are young. For example, four cohorts began in 1967–1968 with young men and women aged 14–24. The next cohort started in 1979 with men and women aged 14–21, who are still being followed today. Another cohort started in 1997 with adolescents aged 12–16. A new cohort is planned for 2026, for which the age range has not yet been determined (but will likely be similar to that of the 1997 cohort);

2. Since these surveys follow people throughout their life course, they are useful indicators of cumulative disadvantage, which is a key feature of structural racism;

3. The annual or biannual data collection in multiple domains enables studies of how racism moves from one set of institutions

to another—for example, education, training, and achievement scores; employment; household, geography, and contextual variables; family background; dating, marriage, cohabitation, sexual activity, pregnancy and fertility, and children; income, assets, and program participation; and attitudes and expectations. However, because this survey is sponsored by the Bureau of Labor Statistics, health has been studied less extensively and crime and substance use have rarely been studied;

4. The oversample of racial/ethnic minorities in the NLSY enables important subgroup analysis in the study of structural racism;

5. Some intergenerational aspects can also be studied; for example, NLSY79 has a companion survey for the children of its female cohort participants, and NLSY97 had a parent survey in the first year of the project; and

6. The sampling design of the NLSY allows for the study of siblings and cousins, with controls for family background.

Nonetheless, several weaknesses have restricted the usefulness of national longitudinal surveys for the study of structural racism, Sanders explained. For example, the NLSY effectively links contextual data spatially but lacks the ability to link data in other dimensions—without school, firm, health care provider, and law enforcement agency IDs, important institutions where structural racism could vary are not considered. Intergenerational data are also limited in the NLSY. Historically, diversity in the planning process and design team has not been a priority for the NLSY, which likely affected survey content and design. He suggested that leadership and collective action could address this weakness, with the research community actively providing input and the Bureau of Labor Statistics staff justifying the content and design decisions. More specific areas of weakness include that although the NLSY has measured outcomes effectively (e.g., when a person was arrested), it has not successfully measured the processes leading to those outcomes (e.g., why the person was arrested). Additionally, because the NLSY is somewhat of a general-purpose survey, content relevant to *all* participants is prioritized over content that might be highly relevant to studies of structural racism but less relevant generally. Furthermore, he continued, although the representative oversamples are useful, a question remains as to whether they are large enough; for example, historically, sample sizes of minorities with high socioeconomic status have been small. Although there have been efforts to collect data specifically on health every 10 years beginning at ages 30 and 40 in the NLSY79 and NLSY97, respectively, the health data are generally weak in the NLSY relative to those in health surveys. He underscored that this is a missed opportunity to observe the effects of structural racism on health that begin far earlier in life. Additionally, although the NLSY97 collects stressors more effectively than the NLSY79, it still does not collect race-specific stressors. No biomarker assessments are included in the NLSY, he continued, and self-reports on biomarkers are limited, which conflates health access with health conditions. Lastly, the NLSY lacks assessments that are typically important in health surveys (e.g., measured height, weight, blood pressure, and pulse, as well as genetic data). However, despite the aforementioned weaknesses, he pointed out that health scientists are the fastest-growing set of NLSY users.

In closing, Sanders detailed the new NLSY cohort, for which the planning process is underway for 2026 data collection. Its planners are prioritizing diversity and engaging a wide set of stakeholders by involving (1) content panels with subject matter experts in family background and cognition, K–12 education and health, the environment, and Department of Defense interests; (2) listening sessions on childhood and family retrospective, mental health, physical health and the environment; (3) listening sessions on innovations in international surveys and the nature of the work, as well as data needs of think tanks, nonprofits, and research organizations; (4) invitations to registered NLSY users to participate in the user survey; and (5) analysis of alternative data sources and underused variables. Sanders expressed his hope that the 2026 NLSY cohort will better meet the needs of a diverse research community and be more impactful for the study of structural racism.

STRENGTHENING INFRASTRUCTURE FOR RESEARCH ON STRUCTURAL RACISM AND AGING

Jennifer Manly (workshop planning committee member and professor of neuropsychology at Columbia University) emphasized that because racism is a "fundamental cause of disease and death" and understanding racism is key to eliminating health inequities, the investigation of the systems that cause harm through structural racism is within the purview of the National Institutes of Health (NIH). Accordingly, NIH has made a commitment to end structural racism in the biomedical research enterprise, which requires robust health equity research (Collins et al., 2021).[1] Manly highlighted a March 2021 NIH-wide call for applications to understand and address the impact of structural racism and discrimination on minority health and health disparities.[2] However, its August 2021 deadline did not provide enough time for researchers without already-funded projects or an existing research infrastructure to submit an R01 with preliminary results.

---

[1] See also https://www.nih.gov/ending-structural-racism/unite
[2] See https://grants.nih.gov/grants/guide/rfa-files/rfa-md-21-004.html

She underscored that this created a significant missed opportunity for many interdisciplinary teams to participate in this important research.

Manly asserted that to build capacity for structural racism research, institutions have to provide resources for assessing and eliminating racism, align promotion and tenure with best practices for health equity, and sustain this commitment over the long term. Furthermore, she continued, an institution's commitment to antiracism should become a score-driving criterion for institutional resources in grants. Part of building this new research infrastructure includes building competencies among research teams to do health equity research within a framework of race-making (historical, dynamic, relational, contextual); creating a score-driving team that represents communities in the study with proven success in community engagement; encouraging personal awareness and adapting behaviors among researchers who might lack appropriate expertise (see Lett et al., 2022); building multidisciplinary teams; and understanding how to prioritize community ownership of research goals, resources, and capacities.

Manly stressed that diversity does not automatically equate with equity, which is an important concept to understand both when forming research teams (Jeske et al., 2022) and when selecting research participants. For instance, recruiting diverse research team members without allowing those individuals to serve in leadership roles or to guide study design does not lead to equitable research. She highlighted the importance of "disrupting the power differential" to better protect Black, Indigenous, and Latinx researchers at all stages of their careers. She added that irresponsible research approaches have lasting impacts.

Manly also noted that "community mistrust of the medical system and of research is not a fundamental driver of health inequalities." To engage communities around Alzheimer's research, for example, Green-Harris and colleagues (2019) incorporated the community's value system in their work, became a part of the "community fabric" by offering services for older adults, met community needs, and established relationships. Manly emphasized that to engage with a community at this level, funding support beyond that of NIH is required. She also suggested that funding not be awarded to teams unwilling to engage with communities. As an example of a successful research project that included interdisciplinary teams and engaged communities in structural racism research, she described the Investment in Communities Offspring Study, to which a social work team was built in to the funded staff to help research participants navigate community resources related to housing, food assistance, and mental health services.

Manly emphasized the need to raise the bar for both research products (see Boyd et al., 2020) and research teams, and indicated that an ahistorical approach to understanding racial health inequalities is unacceptable (see

Williams, 2019). She articulated that a sustainable data infrastructure for structural racism research on health and aging requires:

1. Representative, not convenience, samples (i.e., oversampling techniques reflect heterogeneity within groups);
2. Funding for life-course and longitudinal design;
3. Core support for multiple sources of data (e.g., residential history, individual sources of stress and positive well-being, biomarker collection, in-home assessment, and administrative linkages); and
4. Incentives to focus research frameworks on structural and policy change.

INSIGHTS FROM THE CENTER FOR ANTIRACISM RESEARCH FOR HEALTH EQUITY

Rachel Hardeman (associate professor and Blue Cross endowed professor of health and racial equity in the Division of Health Policy and Management, University of Minnesota School of Public Health) explained that the Center for Antiracism Research for Health Equity (CARHE) pursues health equity and justice for every individual, family, and community in Minnesota and beyond. It works to identify, understand, and dismantle structural racism through multidisciplinary antiracist and collaborative research, education and training, authentic community engagement, and narrative change, as well as by serving as a trusted resource for members of the public health and policy communities. Fostering authentic community engagement and serving as a trusted resource are of particular importance, Hardeman continued. To achieve those two goals, she proposed that multidisciplinary teams engaged in research reflect the communities harmed by structural racism. She asserted that much work remains to measure and combat structural racism as researchers continue to leverage existing expertise and innovation.

Hardeman reflected on the status of naming and measuring structural racism in the public health scholarship. For example, Hardeman and colleagues (2018) found that among all articles published in the top 50 highest-impact public health journals from 2002 to 2015, only 25 articles named "structural," "systemic," or "institutional" racism in the title or abstract. Groos and colleagues (2018) found only 20 articles that included measures of structural racism, and these measures of structural racism were in the following domains: residential housing, social institutions, immigration and border enforcement, political participation, socioeconomic status, criminal justice, and the workplace environment. She pointed out that many of the measures in these 20 articles were chosen by their authors based on the availability of public data, which were then analyzed in the context of differential experiences attributed to structural racism. Hardeman encouraged researchers to continue to leverage available data to move the field forward.

Hardeman remarked that the first step in conducting research on structural racism is to develop an antiracist research framework that centers on (1) the notion that racism is a fundamental cause of health inequities at the margins; (2) the notion that systems, policies, social structures, and history create the conditions that allow inequities to persist; and (3) reconsideration of which evidence is "real." She underscored that researchers should work authentically with communities to cocreate evidence that will dismantle the existing societal structure organized around a "powerful center" and "the margins." She indicated that CARHE held several virtual community conversations with people across varied racial backgrounds to better understand their experiences with structural racism and their thoughts about how it could be measured. These conversations, as well as the work of Chambers and colleagues (2021) on Black women's perspectives in particular, have revealed domains of structural racism that have not yet been captured quantitatively. Moving forward, Hardeman continued, incorporating and leading with community voices can inform the development of a data infrastructure for structural racism measurement. Accordingly, CARHE has an objective to build a nationally, publicly available data repository that could be used by researchers, community members, and policy makers to understand how structural racism is operating and its impact on population health and well-being—The MeasuringRacism Data Portal® (Figure 3-1). This approach centers at the margins, with community voices guiding and holding researchers accountable.

REFLECTIONS AND DISCUSSION

Serving as the discussant for this session of the workshop, Margaret Hicken (workshop planning committee member and research associate professor in the Institute for Social Research at the University of Michigan) highlighted three themes that emerged during the presentations:

1. Data and narrative are influenced by those with power, yet collaborative research includes those who are surveilled in decisions about what information is collected;
2. A very small group determines what is included in large, expensive panel datasets; however, more people could be involved in determining what data are collected and how they are linked; and
3. Gatekeeping continues to be a barrier to funding and publication. Remaining questions include how academic success is defined, who develops research questions, and how those questions are tested.

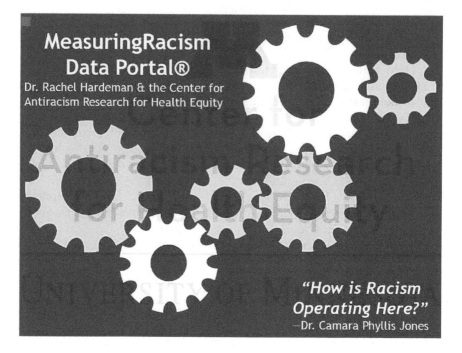

FIGURE 3-1 The MeasuringRacism Data Portal would illuminate how race operates and its impact on population health.
SOURCE: Workshop presentation by Rachel Hardeman, May 17, 2022.

Hicken also identified an overarching theme of the workshop: research teams comprised of scholars with diverse experiences are best suited to understand the drivers of structural racism. She advocated for scholars trained in population health, and thus who are relatively new to this research, to look beyond the scholarship in their own field—humanists, humanistic social scientists, and artists have been studying racism for centuries. She also emphasized the value of expanding place-based research methods, because a place has a "living history" that shapes health variations within and between communities. Neighborhood plays a key role in studies of structural racism, she continued, as residential segregation is a tool for those in power to invest and disinvest in different groups of people.

A participant requested examples of research that has successfully assessed racism at the structural level. Sanders recalled, as one example, the scholarship of presenter Jamein Cunningham (assistant professor in the Jeb E. Brooks School of Public Policy at Cornell University) on how police contracts affect community outcomes. He also championed the use of creative data collection and linkage for nonspatial inequalities and institutions.

Hicken pointed out that no data are perfect and advocated for the use of theory-informed interdisciplinary frameworks for guiding research questions before data are collected and linked.

A participant inquired about specific priorities for data linkage. Manly supported the practice of collecting data on life experiences to better understand a community's residential history (e.g., number of moves people have made as well as the dates they were in certain locations), which enables place-based linkages that could provide additional information about displacement, for instance. She also reflected on the Jackson Heart Study,[3] which asked people about their experiences with stress and racism, as a model of effective survey research. Sanders explained that because all data linkages require informed consent, building trust is the first step in encouraging people to share their personal information with the research community. As an example of creative data linkage, he referenced Lisa Cook's scholarship on the timing and spatial variation in locations of Civil War Confederate statues as a measure of structural racism and its effects on socioeconomic outcomes.

Another participant asked how best to incentivize data sharing. Givens described an ongoing movement toward data transparency, which could motivate more people to recognize that data are a public good not meant to be "held behind walls." Hardeman suggested a focus on "data for action," as well as building infrastructure so that data sharing becomes an easy, trusted process.

A participant posed a question about the future of interdisciplinary training for population health scholars. Givens encouraged researchers to reflect on their identities: honest and difficult conversations are critical in helping people understand how to use their influence in the workforce. Hardeman said that, after this critical self-reflection, if each person enters the training knowing their "why," the training most suitable to achieve this why can be selected. Hicken wondered how to build diverse, interdisciplinary teams when academia remains segregated. Manly inspired researchers to be creative and disruptive: those with tenure and R01 funding could use their privilege and power to change the academic landscape, where "Whiteness is a credential" (Ray, 2019). She stressed that innovation and time, as well as shifts in reviewer and promotion and tenure structures could enable substantive change in recognizing and rewarding diverse teams.

---

[3] See https://www.jacksonheartstudy.org

4

Key Takeaways

Before inviting discussants and speakers to share their key takeaways from the workshop, Hedwig (Hedy) Lee (workshop planning committee chair and professor of sociology at Duke University) reviewed the workshop's guiding question—How can insights be applied regarding the conceptualization, measurement, and modeling of structural racism to inform decisions about:

1. What new measures of structural racism or data linkages could be used in ongoing or future studies helpful to advance aging research;
2. What mechanisms or data linkages could be used in ongoing or future studies that link structural racism to disparities in health and well-being over time and place; and
3. What study designs could be used to consider how structural factors operate to shape health over the life course?

David Takeuchi (workshop planning committee member and professor and associate dean for faculty excellence in the University of Washington School of Social Work) described the notion of "unpacking the other"[1] as essential for structural racism research. He mentioned, as an example of unpacking the other, a National Institute on Aging–funded study[2] of

---

[1] This concept was presented on the first day of the workshop by Desi Small-Rodriguez, assistant professor of sociology and American Indian studies at the University of California, Los Angeles.
[2] See https://reporter.nih.gov/search/1VQG3usGnEqVUEImkbCoSw/project-details/10125509

Vietnamese Americans, the trauma of war, and the implications for cognitive functioning, and advocated for similar studies on how past trauma affects people's lives. He also highlighted the role of gatekeepers (e.g., journal editors, funders, and reviewers) and proposed that academic institutions reduce barriers to innovative research by developing a grant program that would allow people to earn credits for research not normally recognized in the tenure process.

René D. Flores (workshop planning committee member and Neubauer Family assistant professor of sociology at the University of Chicago) summarized that structural inequality is a complex research topic because of different manifestations in subpopulations, as well as different mechanisms across time periods and geographic locations. He also highlighted issues in data availability and data integration—barriers that are often created by disciplinary norms and gatekeepers. He championed the role of theoretical and empirical frameworks that integrate the complexity of structural racism and incentivize theory-making and multimethod interdisciplinary approaches. Furthermore, he reiterated that to understand the production of racial inequalities, researchers should explore race as a fluid, contingent, and socially constructed condition rather than treating it as a fixed independent variable in models.

Margaret Hicken (workshop planning committee member and research associate professor in the Institute for Social Research at the University of Michigan) echoed Flores's statement that structural racism research should be grounded in interdisciplinary research frameworks, which means prioritizing the voices of marginalized scholars, especially those from the humanities, arts, and humanistic social sciences. She emphasized that diverse teams of scholars who are substantially involved in the research process are essential for the future of structural racism research.

Jennifer Manly (workshop planning committee member and professor of neuropsychology at Columbia University) agreed with Hicken that many disciplines should be represented in this complex work and that researchers should be thoughtful about every step of the research process—for example, measurement and modeling follow theory, and community engagement before a grant is funded or a study is designed. She also asserted that incentives would help direct resources to conduct this research effectively and that reviewers (of journals, of funding proposals, and for promotion and tenure) should have the appropriate expertise to recognize the complex nature of structural racism research.

Trevon Logan (workshop planning committee member and Hazel C. Youngberg distinguished professor of economics at The Ohio State University) offered three key takeaways from the workshop: (1) Structural racism is not only a historical process but also a dynamic process with evolving form and function, which is an important consideration for modeling; (2) Since structural racism is relational, modeling could be both unidirectional and bidirectional (i.e., race is both "acted out and acted upon"). He added that race and racism are also experiential (i.e., a 30-year-old Black man has a different experience of racism from a 60-year-old Black man); therefore, a life-course perspective helps to contextualize data; and (3) Instead of allowing the measurement of structural racism to move ahead of the theory, he encouraged researchers to consider what structural racism is before determining how to operationalize it in qualitative and quantitative research. He reiterated that the humanities, a space where oppressed people have been encouraged to share their stories, offer key insights on the building blocks of theory for new structural racism research.

Lee expressed her optimism with recent scholarship on improving population health and reducing disparities. She agreed that more interdisciplinary teams would be beneficial for the field but encouraged scholars first to define what *interdisciplinary* means in the context of specific research. She encouraged researchers to think carefully about who and what are included in the evidence base for studies to avoid furthering racial inequalities. She also echoed the assertion that some of the best work is done "at the fringes"[3] and will not be found in the top population health journals. Lee supported the vision of W.E.B. Du Bois, in particular, who recognized that understanding racism and inequality requires not only data collection and visualization but also an understanding of place and space. To continue to move the population health field forward, she proposed the development of measurement and modeling approaches that avoid replicating efforts and creating new siloes, and she invited workshop speakers to share their visions for the future.

Paris "AJ" Adkins-Jackson (assistant professor in the departments of Epidemiology and Sociomedical Sciences in the Mailman School of Public Health at Columbia University) observed that it can be difficult to think about next steps for the future when issues persist in the present. She cautioned that if researchers continue to begin with a problematic foundation, they cannot move forward. She encouraged researchers instead to create a stable foundation and then collaborate.

Frank Edwards (assistant professor of criminal justice at Rutgers University) explained that when new data products are built on uneven foundations, error is induced with each aggregation to another level. Furthermore, correlations in errors across measures are induced when problematic data sources (e.g., the U.S. Census) continue to be used. He encouraged researchers to consider sources of error from data and to think critically about both uncertainty and data-generating processes, especially when

---

[3] This idea was shared by Courtney Boen, assistant professor of sociology at the University of Pennsylvania, on the second day of the workshop.

making comparisons across time and space. He highlighted opportunities for innovation in methodology, for example by coordinating different types of theoretical and historical assumptions about uncertainty and context.

Seth Sanders (Ronald Ehrenberg professor of economics at Cornell University) remarked that coordination of efforts is essential for substantive change to occur, but that scholars should also have the freedom to pursue questions in the ways that suit them best. Researchers want to capture the benefits that come with approaching problems in different ways while still having a coordinated way forward. Sanders also noted that it might make sense to have interdisciplinary teams at some times but not others; it will depend on the specific question being asked.

A participant posed a question about how White investigators could become more involved in structural racism research without being accused of cultural appropriation. Amy Kate Bailey (associate professor in the Department of Sociology at the University of Illinois Chicago) reflected on her work as a White scholar, which focuses primarily on quantitative historical research of racial violence. She asserted that it is incumbent upon White scholars who do have access to the rooms where decisions are made to use their privilege to ensure that research and research teams are diverse, inclusive, and equitable. Logan added that structural racism research is not just about studying explicitly racialized people because the data-generation process is itself structurally racist. Since everything is a product of a racially structured process, he continued, all people are necessary implicated in the study of structural racism (encompassing, for example, traditional labor economics wage regressions on White working-age males).

Courtney Boen (assistant professor of sociology at the University of Pennsylvania) pointed out that quantitative data are naturally historical and backward-facing. Reflecting on the scholarship of Bruce Western, who noted that quantitative data "hobble our chances at promoting transformative change," Boen said that the path forward has to be visionary. Because limitations in data and methods have political implications that can prevent the realization of true equity and justice, she asserted that rich, descriptive evidence could be leveraged to move the field forward in new ways. Reflecting on programs such as Interdisciplinary Research Leaders[4] and Evidence for Action,[5] Manly encouraged researchers to consider how their work could inform policy and how they could communicate more directly to policy makers. Rachel Hardeman (associate professor and Blue Cross endowed professor of health and racial equity in the Division of Health Policy and Management, University of Minnesota School of Public Health) added that the community voice should be centered in any message crafted

---

[4] See https://interdisciplinaryresearch-leaders.org
[5] See https://www.evidenceforaction.org

for policy makers and cautioned that a policy lever in one direction could impact one in another direction.

Adkins-Jackson urged participants to read the work of legal scholars who have studied race (e.g., John A. Powell and Kimberlé W. Crenshaw) to better conceptualize models for structural racism research in public health, and emphasized that research could be motivated by specific problematic policies or policy interventions. Lee added a suggestion for workshop participants to read Emily Wang's scholarship on transitions clinics for those returning to society after incarceration, as well as the works of James Jackson, Arline Geronimus, and Nancy Krieger; she stressed that the precedents set by their research will help move the public health field forward.

References

Acharya, A., Blackwell, M., and Sen, M. (2016). The political legacy of American slavery. *The Journal of Politics*, 78(3), 621–641.

Adkins-Jackson, P.B., Jackson Preston, P.A., and Hairston, T. (2022). "The only way out": How self-care is conceptualized by Black women. *Ethnicity & Health*, 1–17. https://doi.org/10.1080/13557858.2022.2027878

Adkins-Jackson, P.B., Turner-Musa, J., and Chester, C. (2019). The path to better health for black women: Predicting self-care and exploring its mediating effects on stress and health. *Inquiry*, 56, 1–8. https://doi.org/10.1177/0046958019870968

Aislinn Bohren, J., Hull, P., and Imas, A. (2022). *Systemic discrimination: Theory and measurement*. Working Paper 29820. National Bureau of Economic Research.

Alpert, G.P., and MacDonald, J.M. (2001). Police use of force: An analysis of organizational characteristics. *Justice Quarterly*, 18(2). https://doi.org/10.1080/07418820100094951

Arias, E., Xu, J., Curtin, S., Bastian, B., and Tejana-Vera, B. (2021). Mortality profile of the non-Hispanic American Indian or Alaska Native Population, 2019. *National Vital Statistics Reports*, 70(12). https://stacks.cdc.gov/view/cdc/110370

Ba, B.A., Knox, D., Mummolo, J., and Rivera, R. (2021). The role of officer race and gender in police-civilian interactions in Chicago. *Science*, 371(6530), 696–702. https://doi.org/10.1126/science.abd8694

Bailey, Z.D., Krieger, N., Agenor, M., Graves, J., Linos, N., and Bassett, M.T. (2017). Structural racism and health inequities in the USA: Evidence and interventions. *Lancet*, 389(10077), 1453–1463. https://doi.org/10.1016/S0140-6736(17)30569-X

Baldwin, J. (1984). On being 'white'. . . and other lies. *Essence*.

Battle-Baptiste, W., and Rusert, B., eds. (2018). *W.E.B. Du Bois's Data Portraits: Visualizing Black America—The Color Line at the Turn of the Twentieth Century*. Princeton Architectural Press.

Bembeneck, E., Nissan, R., and Obermeyer, Z. (2021). To stop algorithmic bias, we first have to define it. *Brookings*. https://www.brookings.edu/research/to-stop-algorithmic-bias-we-first-have-to-define-it/

Benjamin, R. (2014). Conjuring difference, concealing inequality: A brief tour of racecraft. *Theory and Society*, 43(6), 638–688.

Bhatt, C.B., and Beck-Sague, C.M. (2018). Medicaid expansion and infant mortality in the United States. *American Journal of Public Health*, 108(4), 565–567. https://doi.org/10.2105/AJPH.2017.304218

Bobo, L., and Kluegel, J.R. (1991). *Whites' stereotypes, social distance, and perceived discrimination toward Blacks, Hispanics and Asians: Toward a multi-ethnic framework.* Paper presented at the 86th Annual Meeting of the American Sociological Association, Cincinnati, OH, August.

Bobo, L.D., Charles, C.Z., Krysan, M., and Simmons, A.D. (2012). The real record on racial attitudes. In P.V. Marsen (Ed.), *Social trends in American Life: Findings from the General Social Survey since 1972*. Princeton University Press.

Boen, C., Graetz, N., Peele, M., Venkataramani, A., and Ortiz, R. Forthcoming. *The scars of legal violence: Restrictive immigration policy, heightened immigration enforcement, and population health inequality.*

Bonilla-Silva, E. (1997). Rethinking racism: Toward a structural interpretation. *American Sociological Review*, 62(3), 465–480. https://doi.org/10.2307/2657316

Bonilla-Silva, E. (2019). Feeling race: Theorizing the racial economy of emotions. *American Sociological Review*, 84(1), 1–25. https://doi.org/10.1177/0003122418816958

Bonilla-Silva, E. (2021). What makes systemic racism systemic? *Sociological Inquiry*, 91(3), 513–533. https://doi.org/10.1111/soin.12420

Bonilla-Silva, E. (2022). *Racism without racists* (6th ed.). Rowman & Littlefield.

Bower, K.M., Geller, R.J., Perrin, N.A., and Alhusen, J. (2018). Experiences of racism and preterm birth: Findings from Pregnancy Risk Assessment Monitoring System, 2004–2012. *Women's Health Issues*, 28(6), 495–501. https://doi.org/10.1016/j.whi.2018.06.002

Boyd, R.W., Lindo, E.G., Weeks, L.D., and McLemore, M.R. (2020). On racism: A new standard for publishing on racial health inequities. *Health Affairs Forefront.* https://doi.org/10.1377/forefront.20200630.939347

Brave Heart, M.Y.H. (1998). The return to the sacred path: Healing the historical trauma and historical unresolved grief response among the Lakota through a psychoeducational group intervention. *Smith College Studies in Social Work*, 68(3), 287–305. https://doi.org/10.1080/00377319809517532

Brave Heart, M.Y.H. (1999). Oyate Ptayela: Rebuilding the Lakota Nation through addressing historical trauma among Lakota parents. *Journal of Human Behavior and the Social Environment*, 2(1/2), 109–126.

Brave Heart, M.Y.H. (2003). The historical trauma response among natives and its relationship with substance abuse: A Lakota illustration. *Journal of Psychoactive Drugs*, 35(1), 7–13. https://doi.org/10.1080/02791072.2003.10399988

Brown, D.A. (2021). *The Whiteness of wealth: How the tax system impoverishes Black Americans—And how we can fix it*. Crown.

Chae, D.H., Clouston, S., Martz, C.D., Hatzenbuehler, M.L., Cooper, H.L.F., Turpin, R., Stephens-Davidowitz, S., and Kramer, M.R. (2018). Area racism and birth outcomes among Blacks in the United States. *Social Science & Medicine*, 199, 49–55. https://doi.org/10.1016/j.socscimed.2017.04.019

Chambers, B.D., Arega, H.A., Arabia, S.E., Taylor, B., Barron, R.G., Gates, B., Scruggs-Leach, L., Scott, K.A., and McLemore, M.R. (2021). Black women's perspectives on structural racism across the reproductive lifespan: A conceptual framework for measurement development. *Maternal and Child Health Journal*, 25(3), 402–413. https://doi.org/10.1007/s10995-020-03074-3

ChangeLab Solutions. (2019). *A blueprint for changemakers: Achieving health equity through law & policy*. https://www.changelabsolutions.org/product/blueprint-changemakers

Chicago Commission on Race Relations. (1922). *The Negro in Chicago: A study of race relations and a race riot*. University of Chicago Press.

Coates, T.-N. (2015). *Between the world and me.* Spiegel & Grau.

Coates, T.-N. (2017). My president was black. *The Atlantic,* January/February.

Collins, W.J., and Margo, R.A. (2003). Race and the value of owner-occupied housing, 1940-1990. *Regional Science and Urban Economics, 33*(3), 255–286.

Collins, F.S., Adams, A.B., Aklin, C., Archer, T.K., Bernard, M.A., Boone, E., Burklow, J., Evans, M.K., Jackson, S., Johnson, A.C., Lorsch, J., Lowden, M.R., Nápoles, A.M., Ordóñez, A.E., Rivers, R., Rucker, V., Schwetz, T., Segre, J.A., Tabak, L.A., Hooper, M.W., Wolinetz, C., and NIH UNITE. (2021). Affirming NIH's commitment to addressing structural racism in the biomedical research enterprise. *Cell, 184*(12), 3075–3079. https://doi.org/10.1016/j.cell.2021.05.014

Conrad, A.H., and Meyer, J.R. (1964). *The economics of slavery.* Aldine Publishing Company.

Cook, L.D. (2014). Violence and economic activity: Evidence from African American patents, 1870-1940. *Journal of Economic Growth, 19*(2), 221–257.

Cook, L.D., Logan, T.D., and Parman, J.M. (2018). Racial segregation and Southern lynching. *Social Science History, 42*(4), 635–675.

Corntassel, J. (2003). Who is Indigenous? "Peoplehood" and ethnonationalist approaches to rearticulating Indigenous identity. *Nationalism and Ethnic Politics, 9*(1), 75–100. https://doi.org/10.1080/13537110412331301365

Cox, R., Cunningham, J.P., and Ortega, A. (2021). The impact of affirmative action litigation on police killings of civilians. http://www.jameinpcunningham.com/uploads/1/1/2/0/112070441/affirmative_action_and_police_killings.pdf

Cox, R., Cunningham, J., Ortega, A., and Whaley, K. (2022). *Black lives: The high cost of segregation.* Presented at the Population Association of American 2022 Annual Meeting, Atlanta, GA.

Crenshaw, K.W., Gotanda, N., Peller, G., and Thomas, K. (Eds.). (1996). *Critical race theory: The key writings that formed the movement.* The New Press.

Cunningham, J., Feir, D., and Gillezeau, R. (2021). *Collective bargaining rights, policing, and civilian deaths.* IZA Institute of Labor Economics Discussion Paper Series, March. https://docs.iza.org/dp14208.pdf

Cunningham, J.P., and Gillezeau, R. (2021). Don't shoot! The impact of historical African American protest on police killings of civilians. *Journal of Quantitative Criminology, 37*(1), 1–34.

Cunningham, D., and Phillips, B.T. (2007). Context for mobilization: Spatial settings and Klan presence in North Carolina, 1964–1966. *American Journal of Sociology, 113*(3), 781–814.

Cunningham, J.P., and Stuart, B. (2022). Racial difference in labor market outcomes and victimization: Evidence from the Great Recession.

Danticat, E. (2016). Message to my daughters. *The fire this time: A new generation speaks about race.* Scribner.

Edwards, F., Lee, H., and Esposito, M. (2019). Risk of being killed by police use of force in the United States by age, race–ethnicity, and sex. *Proceedings of the National Academy of Sciences, 116*(34), 16793–16798. https://doi.org/10.1073/pnas.1821204116

Ellison, R. (1952). *Invisible man.* Random House.

Fadel, L. (Host). (2022, May 9). Examining the many birth disparities in Mississippi, health center CEO says. [Radio broadcast episode]. Morning Edition. https://www.npr.org/2022/05/09/1097540973/there-are-many-birth-disparities-in-mississippi-health-center-ceo-says

Fields, K.E., and Fields, B.J. (2012). *Racecraft: The soul of inequality in American life.* Verso.

Fiske, S.T., and Neuberg, S.L. (1990). A continuum of impression formation, from category-based to individuating processes: Influences of information and motivation on attention and interpretation. *Advances in Experimental Social Psychology, 23*, 1–74. https://doi.org/10.1016/S0065-2601(08)60317-2

Fiske, S.T., Cuddy, A.J.C., Glick, P., and Xu, J. (2002). A model of (often mixed) stereotype content: Competence and warmth respectively follow from perceived status and competition. *Journal of Personality and Social Psychology*, 82(6), 878–902. https://doi.org/10.1037/0022-3514.82.6.878

Fitzgerald, J.A., and Ludeman, W.W. (1926). The intelligence of Indian children. *Journal of Comparative Psychology*, 6(4), 319–328.

Fogel, R.W., and Engerman, S.L. (1974). *Time on the cross: The economics of American slavery*. W.W. Norton & Company, Inc.

Ford, C.L., and Airhihenbuwa, C.O. (2010). The public health critical race methodology: Praxis for antiracism research. *Social Science & Medicine*, 71(8), 1390–1398. https://doi.org/10.1016/j.socscimed.2010.07.030

Garth, T.R. (1931). *Race psychology: A study of racial mental differences*. New York: McGraw Hill.

Gemmill, A., Catalano, R., Casey, J.A., Karasek, D., Alcala, H.E., Elser, H., and Torres, J.M. (2019). Association of preterm births among U.S. Latina women with the 2016 presidential election. *JAMA Network Open*, 2(7), e197084. https://doi.org/10.1001/jamanetworkopen.2019.7084

Ghavami, N., and Peplau, L.A. (2013). An intersectional analysis of gender and ethnic stereotypes testing three hypotheses. *Psychology of Women Quarterly*, 37(1), 113–127. https://doi.org/10.1177/0361684312464203

Givens, M.L., Catlin, B.B., Johnson, S.P., Pollock, E.A., Faust, V.N., Inzeo, P.T., and Kindig, D.A. (2020). What do we know about the drivers of health and equity? A narrative review of graphic representations. *Health Equity*, 4(1), 446–462. https://doi.org/10.1089/heq.2020.0013

Givens, M.L., Gennuso, K.P., Pollock, E.A., and Johnson, S.L. (2021). Deconstructing inequities—Transparent values in measurement and analytic choices. *The New England Journal of Medicine*, 384(19), 1861–1865. https://doi.org/10.1056/NEJMms2035717

Glymour, M.M., and Manly, J.J. (2008). Lifecourse social conditions and racial and ethnic patterns of cognitive aging. *Neuropsychology Review*, 18(3), 223–254. https://doi.org/10.1007/s11065-008-9064-z

Goel, S., Rao, J.M., and Shroff, R. (2016). Precinct or prejudice? Understanding racial disparities in New York City's stop-and-frisk policy. *Annals of Applied Statistics*, 10(1), 365–394.

Graetz, N., Boen, C.E., and Esposito, M.H. (2022). Structural racism and quantitative causal inference: A life course mediation framework for decomposing racial health disparities. *Journal of Health and Social Behavior*, 63(2), 232–249. https://doi.org/10.1177/00221465211066108

Green-Harris, G., Coley, S.L., Koscik, R.L., Norris, N.C., Houston, S.L., Sager, M.A., Johnson, S.C., and Edwards, D.F. (2019). Addressing disparities in Alzheimer's Disease and African-American participation in research: An asset-based community development approach. *Frontiers in Aging Neuroscience*, 11, 125. https://doi.org/10.3389/fnagi.2019.00125

Griffith, D.M., Childs, E.L., Eng, E., and Jeffries, V. (2007). Racism in organizations: The case of a county public health department. *Journal of Community Psychology*, 35(3), 287–302. https://doi.org/10.1002/jcop.20149

Groos, M., Wallace, M., Hardeman, R., and Theall, K.P. (2018). Measuring inequity: A systematic review of methods used to quantify structural racism. *Journal of Health Disparities Research and Practice*, 11(2).

Hardeman, R.R., and Karbeah, J. (2020). Examining racism in health services research: A disciplinary self-critique. *Health Services Research*, 55(S2), 777–780. https://doi.org/10.1111/1475-6773.13558

Hardeman, R.R., Murphy, K.A., Karbeah, J., and Kozhimannil, K.B. (2018). Naming institutionalized racism in the public health literature: A systematic literature review. *Public Health Reports, 133*(3), 240–249. https://doi.org/10.1177/0033354918760574

Hardeman, R.R., Homan, P.A., Chantarat, T., Davis, B.A., and Brown, T.H. (2022). Improving the measurement of structural racism to achieve antiracist health policy. *Health Affairs, 41*(2), 179–186. https://doi.org/10.1377/hlthaff.2021.01489

Hill, C.V., Perez-Stable, E.J., Anderson, N.B., and Bernard, M.A. (2015). The National Institute on Aging Health Disparities Research Framework. *Ethnicity & Disease, 25*(3), 245–254. https://doi.org/10.18865/ed.25.3.245

Holt, T. (2000). *The problem of race in the 21st century.* Cambridge, MA: Harvard University Press.

Holz, J.E., Rivera, R.G., and Ba, B.A. (2019). Spillover effects in police use of force. *Faculty Scholarship at Penn Law,* 2133. https://scholarship.law.upenn.edu/faculty_scholarship/2133/

Howell, E.A., Egorova, N., Balbierz, A., Zeitlin, J., and Hebert, P.L. (2016). Black-white differences in severe maternal morbidity and site of care. *American Journal of Obstetrics and Gynecology, 214*(1), 122.e1.

Jacobs, D., Carmichael, J.T., and Kent, S.L. (2005). Vigilantism, current racial threat, and death sentences. *American Sociological Review, 70*(4), 656–677. https://doi.org/10.1177/000312240507000406

Jacobs, D., Malone, C., and Iles, G. (2012). Race and imprisonments: Vigilante violence, minority threat, and racial politics. *The Sociological Quarterly, 53*(2), 166–187. https://doi.org/10.1111/j.1533-8525.2012.01230.x

Jeske, M., Vasquez, E., Fullerton, S.M., Saperstein, A., Bentz, M., Foti, N., Shim, J.K., and Lee, S.S.-J. (2022). Beyond inclusion: Enacting team equity in precision medicine research. *PLoS One, 17*(2), e0263750. https://doi.org/10.1371/journal.pone.0263750

Johnson, R.B., Onwuegbuzie, A.J., and Turner, L.A. (2007). Toward a definition of mixed methods research. *Journal of Mixed Methods Research, 1*(2), 112–133. https://doi.org/10.1177/1558689806298224

Johnson-Jennings, M., Billiot, S., and Walters, K. (2020). Returning to our roots: Tribal health and wellness through land-based healing. *Genealogy, 4*(3), 91. https://doi.org/10.3390/genealogy4030091

Johnson-Jennings, M.D., Little, M., and Jennings, D. (2019). Indigenous data sovereignty in action: The Food Wisdom Repository. *Journal of Indigenous Wellbeing, 4*(1), 26–38.

Johnson-Jennings, M.D., Belcourt, A., Town, M., Walls, M.L., and Walters, K.L. (2014). Racial discrimination's influence on smoking rates among American Indian Alaska Native two-spirit individuals: Does pain play a role? *Journal of Health Care for the Poor and Underserved, 25*(4), 1667–1678. https://doi.org/10.1353/hpu.2014.0193

Jones, C.P. (2000). Levels of racism: A theoretic framework and a gardener's tale. *American Journal of Public Health, 90*(8), 1212–1215. https://doi.org/10.2105/ajph.90.8.1212

Jones, C.P., Ford, C.L., Griffith, D.M., Bruce, M.A., and Gilbert, K.L. (2019). Action and allegories. In *Racism: Science & tools for the public health professional.* APHA Press. https://doi.org/10.2105/9780875533049ch11

Jussim, L., Eccles, J., and Madon, S. (1996). Social perception, social stereotypes, and teacher expectations: Accuracy and the quest for the powerful self-fulfilling prophecy. *Advances in Experimental Social Psychology, 28*, 281–388. https://doi.org/10.1016/S0065-2601(08)60240-3

Karlins, M., Coffman, T.L., and Walters, G. (1969). On the fading of social stereotypes: Studies in three generations of college students. *Journal of Personality and Social Psychology, 13*(1), 1–16. https://doi.org/10.1037/h0027994

King, R.D., Messner, S.F., and Baller, R.D. (2009). Contemporary hate crimes, law enforcement, and the legacy of racial violence. *American Sociological Review, 74*(2), 291–315.

Kothari, C.L., Paul, R., Dormitorio, B., Ospina, F., James, A., Lenz, D., Baker, K., Curtis, A., and Wiley, J. (2016). The interplay of race, socioeconomic status and neighborhood residence upon birth outcomes in a high Black infant mortality community. *SSM Population Health*, 2, 859–867. https://doi.org/10.1016/j.ssmph.2016.09.011

Kramer, M.R., Cooper, H.L., Drews-Botsch, C.D., Waller, L., and Hogue, C.R. (2010). Metropolitan isolation segregation and Black–White disparities in very preterm birth: A test of mediating pathways and variance explained. *Social Science and Medicine*, 71, 2108–2116. https://doi.org/10.1016/j.socscimed.2010.09.011

Krieger, N. (2019). The U.S. Census and the people's health: Public health engagement from enslavement and "Indians Not Taxed" to census tracts and health equity (1790–2018). *American Journal of Public Health*, 109, 1092–1100. https://doi.org/10.2105/AJPH.2019.305017

Lamont, M. (2009). Responses to racism, health, and social inclusion as a dimension of successful societies. *Successful societies: How institutions and culture affect health*, 151–169. Cambridge University Press.

Laster Pirtle, W.N., and Wright, T. (2021). Structural gendered racism revealed in pandemic times: Intersectional approaches to understanding race and gender health inequities in COVID-19. *Gender & Society*, 35(2), 168–179. https://doi.org/10.1177/08912432211001302

Lawrence, J. (2000). The Indian Health Service and the sterilization of Native American women. *American Indian Quarterly*, 24(3), 400–419.

Lett, E., Adekunle, D., McMurray, P., Ngozi Asabor, E., Irie, W., Simon, M.A., Hardeman, R., and McLemore, M.R. (2022). Health equity tourism: Ravaging the justice landscape. *Journal of Medical Systems*, 46.

Leung, M.W., Yen, I.H., and Minkler, M. (2004). Community based participatory research: A promising approach for increasing epidemiology's relevance in the 21st century. *International Journal of Epidemiology*, 33(3), 499–506. https://doi.org/10.1093/ije/dyh010

Lieberson, S., and Silverman, A.R. (1965). The precipitants and underlying conditions of race riots. *American Sociological Review*, 30(6), 887–898.

Liebler, C.A. (2018). Counting America's first peoples. *Annals of the American Academy of Political and Social Science*, 677(1), 180–190. https://doi.org/10.1177/0002716218766276

Logan, T.D., and Parman, J.M. (2017). The national rise in residential segregation. *Journal of Economic History*, 77(1), 127–170.

Lukes, S. (2005). *Power: A radical view* (2nd ed.). Red Globe Press.

Masera, F. (2021). Violent crime and the overmilitarization of U.S. policing. *Journal of Law, Economics, and Organization*, 37(3), 479–511. https://doi.org/10.1093/jleo/ewaa021

Mayorga-Gallo, S. (2014). *Behind the white picket fence: Power and privilege in a multiethnic neighborhood*. The University of North Carolina Press.

Mbembe, A. (2003). Necropolitics. *Public Culture*, 15(1), 11–40.

McAdam, D., Snellman, K., and Su, Y. (2013). *"Burning down the house": Race, politics, the media, and the burning of churches in the U.S., 1996–2001*. Unpublished manuscript.

Menifield, C.E., Shin, G., and Strother, L. (2019). Do white law enforcement officers target minority suspects? *Public Administration Review*, 79(1), 56–68. https://doi.org/10.1111/puar.12956

Messner, S.F., Deane, G.D., Anselin, L., and Pearson-Nelson, B. (2005). Locating the vanguard in rising and falling homicide rates across U.S. cities. *Criminology*, 43(3), 661–696.

Morrison, T. (1998). Home. In W. Lubiano (Ed.), *The house that race built*. Vintage Books.

National Institute on Aging and National Advisory Council on Aging. (2019). *2019 BSR review committee report*. Revised December 16, 2019. https://www.nia.nih.gov/sites/default/files/2020-02/2019-BSR-Review-Committee-Report-508.pdf

Ncube, C.N., Enquobahrie, D.A., Albert, S.M., Herrick, A.L., and Burke, J.G. (2016). Association of neighborhood context with offspring risk of preterm birth and low birthweight: A systematic review and meta-analysis of population-based studies. *Social Science & Medicine, 153,* 156–164. https://doi.org/10.1016/j.socscimed.2016.02.014

Novak, N.L., Geronimus, A.T., and Martinez-Cardoso, A.M. (2017). Change in birth outcomes among infants born to Latina mothers after a major immigration raid. *International Journal of Epidemiology, 46*(3), 839–849. https://doi.org/10.1093/ije/dyw346

O'Connell, H.A. (2012). The impact of slavery on racial inequality in poverty in the contemporary U.S. South. *Social Forces, 90*(3), 713–734. https://doi.org/10.1093/sf/sor021

Office of Management and Budget. (1997). Revisions to the Standards for the Classification of Federal Data on Race and Ethnicity. https://obamawhitehouse.archives.gov/omb/fedreg_1997standards

Onwuegbuzie, A.J., and Collins, K.M.T. (2007). A typology of mixed methods sampling designs in social science research. *The Qualitative Report, 12*(2), 281–316.

Orchard, J., and Price, J. (2017). County-level racial prejudice and the black-white gap in infant health outcomes. *Social Science & Medicine, 181,* 191–198. https://doi.org/10.1016/j.socscimed.2017.03.036

Owens, P.B., Cunningham, D., and Ward, G. (2015). Threat, competition, and mobilizing structures: Motivational and organizational contingencies of the Civil Rights-era Ku Klux Klan. *Social Problems, 62*(4), 572–604. https://doi.org/10.1093/socpro/spv016

Owens, E., Weisburd, D., Amendola, K.L, and Alpert, G.P. (2018). Can you build a better cop? Experimental evidence on supervision, training, and policing in the community. *Criminology & Public Policy, 17*(1), 41–87. https://doi.org/10.1111/1745-9133.12337

Pedulla, D.S. (2014). The positive consequences of negative stereotypes: Race, sexual orientation, and the job application process. *Social Psychology Quarterly, 77*(1), 75–94. https://doi.org/10.1177/0190272513506229

Petteway, R.J. (2022). Something something something by race, 2021. *International Journal of Epidemiology.* https://doi.org/10.1093/ije/dyac010

Phelan, J.C., and Link, B.G. (2013). Fundamental cause theory. *Medical sociology on the move: New directions in theory,* 105–124. Dordrecht: Springer.

Phelan, J.C., and Link, B.G. (2015). Is racism a fundamental cause of inequalities in health? *Annual Review of Sociology, 41,* 311–330. https://doi.org/10.1146/annurev-soc-073014-112305

Pierson, E., Cutler, D.M., Leskovec, J., Mullainathan, S., and Obermeyer, Z. (2021). An algorithmic approach to reducing unexplained pain disparities in underserved populations. *Nature Medicine, 27*(1), 136–140. https://doi.org/10.1038/s41591-020-01192-7

Porter, J.R., Howell, F.M., and Hempel, L.M. (2014). Old times are not forgotten: The institutionalization of segregationist academies in the American South. *Social Problems, 61*(4), 576–601. https://doi.org/10.1525/sp.2014.11155

Public Health Scotland. (2016). *What are health inequalities?* Last updated: December 24, 2021. http://www.healthscotland.scot/health-inequalities/what-are-health-inequalities

Rankine, C. (2015). The condition of black life is one of mourning. *New York Times Magazine,* June 22.

Ransom, R.L., and Sutch, R. (1977). *One kind of freedom: The Economic consequences of emancipation.* Cambridge University Press.

Ray, V. (2019). A theory of racialized organizations. *American Sociological Review, 84*(1), 26–53. https://doi.org/10.1177/0003122418822335

Rodriguez-Lonebear, D. (2021). The blood line: Racialized boundary making and citizenship among Native nations. *Sociology of Race and Ethnicity,* 1–16. https://doi.org/10.1177/2332649220981589

Rozema, K., and Schanzenbach, M. (2019). Good cop, bad cop: Using civilian allegations to predict police misconduct. *American Economic Journal: Economic Policy*, *11*(2), 225–268.

Schachter, A. (2021). Intersecting boundaries: Comparing stereotypes of Native- and foreign-born members of ethnoracial groups. *Social Forces*, *100*(2), 506–539. https://doi.org/10.1093/sf/soab004

Schulz, A., and Northridge, M.E. (2004). Social determinants of health: Implications for environmental health promotion. *Health Education & Behavior*, *31*(4), 455–471. https://doi.org/10.1177/1090198104265598

Schut, R., and Boen, C. Forthcoming. *The effect of immigration policies and enforcement on healthcare access among immigrant agricultural workers, 1989-2018.*

Schwartz, S., Prins, S.J., Campbell, U.B., and Gatto, N.M. (2016). Is the "well-defined intervention assumption" politically conservative? *Social Science and Medicine*, *166*, 254–257. https://doi.org/10.1016/j.socscimed.2015.10.054

Siddiqi, A., Jones, M.K., Bruce, D.J., and Erwin, P.C. (2016). Do racial inequities in infant mortality correspond to variations in societal conditions? A study of state-level income inequality in the U.S., 1992–2007. *Social Science & Medicine*, *164*, 49–58. https://doi.org/10.1016/j.socscimed.2016.07.013

Smith, L.T. (2021). *Decolonizing methodologies: Research and Indigenous peoples* (3rd ed.). Zed Books.

Snipp, C.M. (1989). *American Indians: The first of this land.* Russel Sage Foundation.

Stashko, A., and Garro, H. (2021). *Prosecutor elections and police accountability.* Working paper.

University of Wisconsin Population Health Institute. (2019). *Mobilizing Action Toward Community Health (MATCH).* https://uwphi.pophealth.wisc.edu

Vigdor, J.L., and Glaeser, E.L. (2012). The end of the segregated century: Racial separation in America's neighborhoods, 1890-2010. *Manhattan Institute*, January 22.

Ward, G., Petersen, N., Kupchik, A., and Pratt, J. (2021). Historic lynching and corporal punishment in contemporary southern schools. *Social Problems*, *68*(1), 41–62. https://doi.org/10.1093/socpro/spz044

Williams, D.T. (2019). A call to focus on racial domination and oppression: A response to "Racial and Ethnic Inequality in Poverty and Affluence, 1959–2015." *Population Research and Policy Review*, *38*, 655–663.

Williams, J., and Romer, C. (2020). Black deaths at the hands of law enforcement are linked to historical lynchings. *Economic Policy Institute Working Economics Blog*, June 5.

Williams, M.C., Jr., Weil, N., Rasich, E.A., Ludwig, J., Chang, H., and Egrari, S. (2021). *Body-worn cameras in policing: Benefits and costs.* Working Paper 28622. National Bureau of Economic Research. https://doi.org/10.3386/w28622

Williams, J., Cunningham, J., Bjuggren, C.M., Cox, R., Cook, L., and Logan, T., (2022). *The legacy of lynchings and state-sanctioned violence against Black Americans.* Working paper.

Zou, L.X., and Cheryan, S. (2017). Two axes of subordination: A new model of racial position. *Journal of Personality and Social Psychology*, *112*(5), 696–717. https://doi.org/10.1037/pspa0000080

Appendix A

Workshop Agenda

**WORKSHOP ON STRUCTURAL RACISM AND
RIGOROUS MODELS OF SOCIAL INEQUITY**

National Academy of Sciences Building
2101 Constitution Avenue, NW
Washington, DC 20418

May 16–17, 2022
Room 120

Structural racism refers to the public and private policies, institutional practices, norms, and cultural representations that inherently procure unequal freedom, opportunity, value, resources, advantage, restrictions, constraints, or disadvantage to individuals and populations according to their race or ethnicity both across the life course and between generations. The purpose of this workshop is to identify and discuss the sources and mechanisms through which structural racism operates. Invited experts will not only provide insights into known sources of structural racism and models of health equity, but also go beyond these to discuss novel sources and approaches. The workshop will help identify key research and data needs and priorities for future work on structural racism and health inequity.

After the workshop, the National Academies Press will publish a rapporteur-prepared proceedings volume that summarizes the workshop presentations and discussions.

Support for this workshop is provided by the National Institute on Aging.

DAY 1: Monday, May 16, 2022
10:00 am – 4:00 pm

10:00–10:30 am   **WELCOME AND INTRODUCTIONS**
Malay Majmundar, *Director*, Committee on Population
Frank Bandiera, National Institute on Aging, Division
of Behavioral and Social Research
Hedwig (Hedy) Lee, Department of Sociology, Washington
University in St. Louis

Review of Core Guiding Question for Workshop, (*Chair, Workshop Steering Committee*)
How can we apply insights regarding conceptualization, measurement, and modeling of structural racism to inform decisions about:
1. what new measures of structural racism we ought to collect (or what data linkages are needed) in ongoing or future studies to help advance aging research;
2. what are the mechanisms we ought to collect (or what data linkages are needed) in ongoing or future studies that link structural racism to disparities in health and well-being over time and place;
3. what study designs can be used to study how structural factors operate to shape health over the life course?

10:30 am –   **SESSION 1: Setting the Foundation: Studying Race and**
12:30 pm   **Structural Racism Responsibly**
There has been increasing interest in population and population health research in the measurement of structural racism and its role in a multitude of outcomes over the life course. However, work in this area requires a grounding in foundational work in the humanities and humanistic social sciences on race, race-making, and racism that has been ongoing since the turn of the century (e.g., work of W.E.B. Dubois). In this session, experts in the study of race and racism will provide key insights that are required to ensure that future life-course and aging population health research acknowledges and understands the complexity of these concepts and applies them to data collection and analysis to move the needle in improving population health and well-being and reducing health disparities

10:30   Speaker Talks (15 minutes each)

What is Race and Race-Making? How is Race Used to Control Populations?
Stephanie Li, Washington University in St. Louis, Lynne Cooper Harvey Distinguished Professor of English
Evelynn Hammonds, Barbara Gutmann Rosenkrantz Professor of the History of Science, Professor of African and African American Studies, Harvard University; Professor in the Department of Social and Behavioral Sciences, Harvard T.H. Chan School of Public Health *[VIRTUAL]*

The Many Faces of Racism: What is Structural Racism? Embracing the Complexity of Structural Racism; Understanding the Interlocking Roles and Features of Cultural and Structural Racism

How should we understand and conceptualize the many faces of racism?
Eduardo Bonilla-Silva, James B. Duke Distinguished Professor of Sociology, Duke University *[VIRTUAL]*

How have we understood, measured, and modeled racism in population health and aging research and how does this align with conceptualizations of racism?
Margaret Hicken, Research Associate Professor, Institute for Social Research, University of Michigan *(Member, Workshop Steering Committee) [VIRTUAL]*

11:30	Discussant Questions and Reflections **Trevon Logan,** Hazel C. Youngberg Distinguished Professor of Economics, Ohio State University *(Member, Workshop Steering Committee)*
11:40	BREAK
11:50	General Discussion
12:30–1:30 pm	LUNCH

1:30 – 4:00   **SESSION 2: Assessing the Landscape: The Measurement and Modeling of Structural Racism (Part I)**

Many researchers have developed unique and rigorous measurement and modeling approaches to capture the complexity of structural racism that are theoretically driven and have implications for population health and well-being across the life course. In this session, experts will discuss the different approaches they have used to measure structural racism (e.g., laws, policies, institutions) and model structural racism (e.g., causal models, cumulative impacts) and the consequences of structural racism. The experts will describe the mechanisms that link structural racism to disparities in health and well-being across the life course. They will also consider the strengths and weaknesses of these approaches for population health and aging research.

1:30   Speaker Talks (15 minutes each)
Experimental Design
René D. Flores, Neubauer Family Assistant Professor of Sociology, University of Chicago *(Member, Workshop Steering Committee) [VIRTUAL]*

Quasi-Experimental Approaches
Jamein Cunningham, Assistant Professor, Department of Policy Analysis and Management, Cornell University

Quantitative Historical Data
Amy Kate Bailey, Associate Professor, Department of Sociology, University of Illinois Chicago *[VIRTUAL]*

Data for Understudied Populations
Desi Small-Rodriguez, Assistant Professor of Sociology and American Indian Studies, University of California, Los Angeles *[VIRTUAL]*

Machine Learning
Ziad Obermeyer, Blue Cross of California Distinguished Associate Professor of Health Policy and Management, University of California, Berkeley, School of Public Health *[VIRTUAL]*

2:45   Discussant Questions and Reflections
                David Takeuchi, Professor and Associate Dean for
                Faculty Excellence, University of Washington School of
                Social Work *(Member, Workshop Steering Committee)*
                [VIRTUAL]

3:00   BREAK

3:10   General Discussion

4:00   Day 1 Adjournment

                DAY 2: Tuesday, May 17, 2022
                9:00 am – 3:00 pm

9:00 am   Brief Introduction to Day 2

9:10 – 11:00   **SESSION 3: Assessing the Landscape: The Measurement
                and Modeling of Structural Racism (PART II)**

9:10   Speaker Talks (15 minutes each)

                Mixed Methods Approaches
                Paris "AJ" Adkins-Jackson, Assistant Professor, De-
                partments of Epidemiology and Sociomedical Sciences,
                Mailman School of Public Health, Columbia University

                Place-Based Approaches
                Michelle Johnson-Jennings, Professor and Director of
                Environmentally-based Health & Land-based Healing,
                University of Washington School of Social Work

                Novel Approaches to Survey Data
                Courtney Boen, Assistant Professor of Sociology, Uni-
                versity of Pennsylvania

                Novel Approaches to Administrative and Crowd-
                Sourced Data
                Frank Edwards, Assistant Professor of Criminal Justice,
                Rutgers University

10:10   Discussant Questions and Reflections
René D. Flores, Neubauer Family Assistant Professor of Sociology, University of Chicago (Member, Workshop Steering Committee) *[VIRTUAL]*

10:20   General Discussion

11:00   BREAK

11:15 am–   **SESSION 4: Moving Forward: Data Infrastructure Needs**
12:50 pm   **in Harnessing Data for Research in Structural Racism**
In this session, experts will discuss the data necessary to not only measure and model structural racism, but also identify and measure the mechanisms that link racism to population health and well-being over time, with a focus on aging.

11:15   Speaker Talks (15 minutes each)
Marjory Givens, Associate Director, University of Wisconsin Population Health Institute; CoDirector County Health Rankings & Roadmaps *[VIRTUAL]*

Seth Sanders, Ronald Ehrenberg Professor of Economics, Cornell University *[VIRTUAL]*

Jennifer Manly, Professor of Neuropsychology, Columbia University (*Member, Workshop Steering Committee*) *[VIRTUAL]*

12:00   Insights from the Center for Antiracism Research for Health Equity
Rachel Hardeman, Associate Professor and Blue Cross Endowed Professor of Health and Racial Equity, Division of Health Policy and Management, University of Minnesota School of Public Health *[VIRTUAL]*

12:10   Discussant Questions and Reflections
Margaret Hicken, Research Associate Professor, Institute for Social Research, University of Michigan *(Member, Workshop Steering Committee)* *[VIRTUAL]*

12:20	General Discussion
1:00 – 2:00	LUNCH
2:00 – 3:00	**CLOSING SESSION: The Future Agenda: A Round-Robin Discussion of Key Takeaways**
3:00	Meeting Adjournment

Appendix B

Biographical Information for Workshop Presenters and Discussants

Paris "AJ" Adkins-Jackson is a multidisciplinary, community-partnered health equity researcher and assistant professor in the departments of Epidemiology and Sociomedical Sciences in the Mailman School of Public Health at Columbia University. Adkins-Jackson's research investigates the role of structural racism on healthy aging for historically marginalized populations, such as Black and Pacific Islander communities. Her primary project examines the role of life-course adverse community-level policing exposure on psychological well-being, cognitive function, and biological aging for Black and Latinx/a/o older adults. Her secondary project tests the effectiveness of an antiracist, multilevel, preintervention restorative program to increase community health and institutional trustworthiness through multisector community-engaged partnerships. Adkins-Jackson is a board member of the Society for the Analysis of African American Public Health Issues. She earned a Ph.D. in psychometrics at Morgan State University.

Amy Kate Bailey is associate professor of sociology and fellow of the Institute for Health Research and Policy at the University of Illinois Chicago. Her research interrogates historical racial violence, with a particular focus on the people who were victimized and the contemporary consequences of racial terror. To further this work, she has created multiple datasets using archival data. Bailey's scholarship has been funded by the National Science Foundation and the National Institutes of Health (NIH), and appeared in journals including the *American Journal of Sociology, American Sociological Review, Annals of the American Academy of Political and Social*

Sciences, Population Research and Policy Review, and *Sociology of Race and Ethnicity.* Her book *Lynched: The Victims of Southern Mob Violence,* coauthored with Stewart E. Tolnay, received the 2015 IPUMS Research Award. Bailey previously held a faculty appointment at Utah State University, and was an NIH postdoctoral research fellow at Princeton's Office of Population Research. She earned her B.A. in women's studies and health at the University of California, Santa Cruz, and her M.A. and Ph.D. in sociology at the University of Washington.

Courtney Boen is assistant professor and Axilrod faculty fellow in the Department of Sociology and the Graduate Group in Demography at the University of Pennsylvania. She is also a research associate in the Penn Population Studies Center and Population Aging Research Center; a senior fellow in the Leonard Davis Institute for Health Economics; and an affiliate in the Center for the Study of Ethnicity, Race, and Immigration. Boen's research combines critical and relational theories of race and racism, insights from the life-course perspective, and a variety of social demographic techniques to document and interrogate the patterns and determinants of population health inequities. Her current research focuses on the structural and institutional factors producing racialized inequities in health and mortality, including projects on the roles of immigration policy and surveillance, as well as policing and carceral punishment, in generating and maintaining racialized health inequities. Boen's work has been published in the *Proceedings of the National Academy of Sciences, Social Science and Medicine,* and the *Journal of Health and Social Behavior,* among others. She received her Ph.D. in sociology from the University of North Carolina at Chapel Hill.

Eduardo Bonilla-Silva is James B. Duke distinguished professor of sociology at Duke University. He works in the field of racial/ethnic stratification and has written on racial theory, race and methodology, race in the academy, and the future of racial stratification in the United States. Bonilla-Silva is best known for his book *Racism without Racists,* in which he showed that the language and tropes used to explain away the significance of race amount to a new ideology that he labels *color-blind racism.* He served as president of the American Sociological Association and the Southern Sociological Society in 2018, and has received numerous awards, including the prestigious ASA W.E.B. Du Bois Career of Distinguished Scholarship Award in 2021. Bonilla-Silva received his M.A. and Ph.D. from the University of Wisconsin, but developed his sociological imagination in The University of Puerto Rico, Rio Piedras, where he received a B.A.

Jamein P. Cunningham is assistant professor in the Jeb E. Brooks School of Public Policy at Cornell University. He held previous positions as assistant professor in the economics departments at the University of Memphis and Portland State University, where he taught urban economics, econometrics, labor economics, and Race & Ethnicity in the Economy. Cunningham is an applied microeconometrician with a research interest in demography, crime, and poverty. His research agenda currently consists of four broad, overarching themes focusing on legal aid and access to social justice, as well as how laws, regulations, and federal interventions influence individuals' economic outcomes from marginalized communities. He was a recipient of the Rackham Merit Fellowship and the Eunice Kennedy Shriver National Institute in Child Health and Development Fellowship. Cunningham holds professional memberships in the American Economic Association; the American Law and Economics Association; the Economic History Association; the Racial Democracy, Crime, and Justice Network; and the National Economic Association. He earned a B.A. from Michigan State University, an M.S. from the University of North Texas, and a Ph.D. from the University of Michigan, all in economics.

Frank Edwards is a sociologist broadly interested in social control, the welfare state, racism, and applied statistics. He is assistant professor of criminal justice at Rutgers University-Newark. Edwards' work explores the causes and consequences of the social distribution of state violence. His research has been published in the *Proceedings of the National Academy of Sciences*, *American Sociological Review*, *American Journal of Public Health*, and other outlets. His research has been covered in *The New York Times*, *The Washington Post*, *The Los Angeles Times*, and *PBS News Hour*, among others. He received his Ph.D. in sociology from the University of Washington.

René D. Flores is Neubauer Family assistant professor of sociology at the University of Chicago. His research interests are in the fields of international migration, race and ethnicity, and social stratification, exploring the emergence of social boundaries around immigrants and racial minorities across the world, as well as how these boundaries contribute to the reproduction of ethnic-based social inequality. His work has appeared in the *American Journal of Sociology*, the *American Sociological Review*, *Social Forces*, and *Social Problems*, among others. Flores serves on the editorial boards of the *American Sociological Review* and the *American Journal of Sociology*. He is a member of the Diversity, Equity, and Inclusion Executive Committee of the Population Association of America. He received his Ph.D. in sociology and social policy from Princeton University in 2014. He was the Robert Wood Johnson Foundation scholar in health policy research at the University of Michigan's School of Public Health.

Marjory Givens is associate director of the University of Wisconsin Population Health Institute, codirector of the County Health Rankings & Roadmaps program, and assistant professor of population health sciences. For nearly two decades, Givens has worked to make health and equity routine considerations in shaping the places where people live, learn, work, and play. She has conducted public health research in laboratory and community-based settings, ranging from investigations using biomedical models to health impact assessments and evaluation of community interventions. Givens received a Ph.D. in biomedical sciences from the University of California, San Diego, and an M.S.P.H. in environmental/occupational health and epidemiology from Emory University. She completed postdoctoral training as a health disparities research scholar and was a population health service fellow, both while at the University of Wisconsin–Madison.

Evelynn M. Hammonds is Barbara Gutmann Rosenkrantz professor of the history of science, professor of African and African American studies, chair of the Department of the History of Science, and professor in the Department of Social and Behavioral Sciences at Harvard T.H. Chan School of Public Health, where she has been on the faculty for more than 20 years. Her research focuses on the history of scientific, medical, and sociopolitical concepts of race and gender in the United States. She also works on projects to improve the representation of women of color in STEM fields. Hammonds is currently vice president–elect of the History of Science Society. She is a member of the Committee on Women in Science, Engineering, and Medicine, and of the Roundtable on Black Men and Women in Science, Engineering, and Medicine; and co-chair of the *Transforming Trajectories for Women of Color in Tech* report, all for the National Academies of Sciences, Engineering, and Medicine. She was elected to the National Academy of Medicine and the American Academy of Arts and Sciences, and holds honorary degrees from Spelman and Bates Colleges. Hammonds holds undergraduate degrees in physics from Spelman College and electrical engineering from Georgia Tech, and she earned the S.M. in physics from the Massachusetts Institute of Technology. She earned her Ph.D. in the Department of the History of Science at Harvard University and was a postdoctoral fellow at the Institute for Advanced Study at Princeton University.

Rachel Hardeman is a tenured associate professor in the Division of Health Policy & Management at the University of Minnesota School of Public Health, Blue Cross endowed professor in health and racial equity, founding director of the Center for Antiracism Research for Health Equity, and member of the advisory committee to the director of the Centers for Disease Control and Prevention in 2021. A reproductive health equity researcher, Hardeman applies the tools of population health science and health services research to elucidate a critical and complex determinant of health inequity—racism. She leverages the frameworks of critical race theory and reproductive justice to inform her equity-centered work, which aims to build the empirical evidence of racism's impact on health, particularly for Black birthing people and their babies. Her work also examines the potential mental health impacts for Black birthing people when living in a community that has experienced the killing of an unarmed Black person by police. Published in journals such as the *New England Journal of Medicine* and the *American Journal of Public Health*, Hardeman's research has elicited important conversations on the topics of culturally centered care, police brutality, and structural racism as a fundamental cause of health inequities. Her overarching goal is to contribute to a body of knowledge that links structural racism to health in a tangible way; identifies opportunities for intervention; and dismantles the systems, structures, and institutions that allow inequities to persist. Hardeman received her Ph.D. in health services research and policy from the University of Minnesota School of Public Health.

Margaret Hicken is a tenured research associate professor at the Institute for Social Research at the University of Michigan, where she leads several projects funded by the National Institutes of Health to examine the role of structural racism in population health inequities. Specifically, Hicken examines the interactive roles of historical and contemporary racial residential segregation, and social and toxicant exposures on contemporary population health inequities. Furthermore, she links these exposures to health through potential biological mechanisms, including DNA methylation and other biomarkers, and examines the interactive role of social and genetic risk on population health. Hicken is trained as a social demographer and social epidemiologist, with further training in statistical and population genetics through a 5-year career development award from the National Institutes of Health. She earned a Ph.D. from the University of Michigan.

Michelle Johnson-Jennings is professor and director of the Division of Environmentally Based Health & Land-based Healing at the Indigenous Wellness Research Institute. She holds a joint appointment at the University of Colorado School of Public Health. Johnson-Jennings was associate professor in community health and epidemiology in medicine and associate professor in Indigenous studies, as well as scientific director of the National Indigenous HIV/AIDS Centre at the University of Saskatchewan. Her research interests include Indigenous health and psychology, epidemiology, addiction medicine, and psychological and behavioral aspects of health care. Her therapeutic expertise lies in working with Indigenous communities and decolonizing healing while rewriting narratives of trauma through land-based healing. Johnson-Jennings has partnered with many international and national Indigenous nations, organizations, and communities to prevent substance abuse, food addiction, and obesity. She received her doctoral degree in counseling psychology from the University of Wisconsin–Madison in 2010.

Hedwig (Hedy) Lee is professor of sociology at Duke University and visiting professor in the Department of Sociology at Washington University in St. Louis. She is interested broadly in the social determinants and consequences of population health and health disparities in the United States, with a particular focus on the role of structural racism in racial/ethnic health disparities. Lee's work examines the impact of family member incarceration on the health of family members, the association between racialized chronic stress and mental/physical health, the trends in racial/ethnic health disparities, and the role of histories of racial violence in racial/ethnic health disparities. As an interdisciplinary scholar, her articles span a range of topics and disciplines, including demography, medicine, political science, public health, social work, and sociology. Lee serves on the board of the Population Association of America and the research advisory board for the Vera Institute for Justice. She is also a member of the General Social Survey Board of Overseers and a member of the National Academies of Sciences, Engineering, and Medicine's Committee on Population. Lee has a Ph.D. in sociology from the University of North Carolina at Chapel Hill.

Stephanie Li is Lynne Cooper Harvey distinguished professor of English at Washington University in St. Louis. Her first monograph, *Something Akin to Freedom: The Choice of Bondage in Narratives by African American Women*, analyzes literary examples in which African American women decide to remain within or enter into conditions of bondage. Her next book, *Signifying without Specifying: Racial Discourse in the Age of Obama*, describes a new mode of racial discourse for the 21st century, in what Toni Morrison calls "race-specific, race-free language." Her interest in Obama's writings led her to guest coedit, with Professor Gordon Hutner, the fall 2012 special issue of *American Literary History*, entitled "Writing the Presidency." Her third monograph, *Playing in the White: Black Writers, White Subjects*, considers how postwar African American authors represent Whiteness. Her most recent book, *Pan–African American Literature: Signifyin(g) Immigrants in the Twenty-First Century*, is dedicated to charting the contours of Pan–African American literature. She has also written two short biographies of Toni Morrison and Zora Neale Hurston, and is currently at work on a monograph entitled *Ugly White People*. She earned a Ph.D. in English language and literature from Cornell University.

Trevon D. Logan is Hazel C. Youngberg Trustees distinguished professor of economics and associate dean in the College of Arts and Sciences at The Ohio State University. He is a research associate in the Development of the American Economy Program and the director of the Race and Stratification in the Economy Working Group at the National Bureau of Economic Research. A former president of the National Economic Association and member of the American Economic Association's Committee on the Status of the Minority Groups in the Economics Profession, Logan is currently codirector of the American Economic Association's Mentoring Program and member of the editorial boards of the *Journal of Economic Literature* and the *Journal of Economic Perspectives*. His current research focuses on racial inequality and economic history. Logan was named by *Fortune Magazine* as "One of the 19 Black Economists You Should Know and Celebrate" in 2020. He is currently a member of the National Academies of Sciences, Engineering, and Medicine's planning committee Strengthening the Evidence Base to Improve Economic and Social Mobility in the United States, and a member of the Committee on Population. Logan received a B.S. in economics from the University of Wisconsin–Madison, master's degrees in demography and economics from the University of California, Berkeley, and a Ph.D. in economics from University of California, Berkeley.

Jennifer J. Manly is professor of neuropsychology at the Gertrude H. Sergievsky Center and the Taub Institute at Columbia University. Her research on cultural, medical, and genetic predictors of cognitive aging and Alzheimer's disease among African Americans and Hispanics has been funded by the National Institute on Aging and the Alzheimer's Association. Manly has authored more than 100 peer-reviewed publications, as well as eight chapters in edited books. She aims to improve the diagnostic accuracy of neuropsychological tests in detecting cognitive impairment and Alzheimer's disease among African American and Hispanic elders. Her recent work focuses on the specificity of cognitive tasks in detecting subtle cognitive decline among illiterate and low-literacy older adults, with important implications for determining the complex influence of reading and writing skills on brain function. Manly is a current member of the National Academies of Sciences, Engineering, and Medicine's Committee on Population. She has a Ph.D. in clinical psychology from the University of California, San Diego. After a clinical internship at Brown University, Manly completed a postdoctoral fellowship at Columbia University.

Ziad Obermeyer is associate professor and Blue Cross of California distinguished professor at the University of California, Berkeley, where he conducts research and teaches at the intersection of machine learning and health. He is cofounder of Nightingale Open Science, a nonprofit that makes massive new medical imaging datasets available for research, as well as Dandelion, a platform for artificial intelligence innovation in health. Obermeyer is a Chan Zuckerberg biohub investigator and a faculty research fellow at the National Bureau of Economic Research, and was named an Emerging Leader by the National Academy of Medicine. Previously, he was a consultant at McKinsey & Co. and an assistant professor at Harvard Medical School. He continues to practice emergency medicine in underserved communities. Obermeyer's papers appear in a wide range of journals, including *Science*, *Nature Medicine*, the *New England Journal of Medicine*, the *Journal of the American Medical Association*, and the *Proceedings of the International Conference on Machine Learning*, and have won awards from professional societies in medicine and economics. His work on algorithmic bias is frequently cited in the public debate about artificial intelligence, and in federal and state regulatory guidance and investigations. Obermeyer holds an M.D. from Harvard Medical School.

Seth Sanders is Ronald Ehrenberg professor of economics at Cornell University. Prior to joining the faculty at Cornell, he was professor of economics and public policy at Duke University and director of the Duke Population Research Institute. His scholarly work has covered a range of topics in labor economics and economic demography, including aging and cognition, race and gender gaps in earnings among the highly educated, the effects of extreme economic changes on workers and families, the performance of gay and lesbian families in the economy, and the economic consequences of teenage childbearing. Sanders was research director of the first Census research data center at Carnegie Mellon University. He has worked with restricted-use Census data throughout his career, including current work on the Core Longitudinal Infrastructure Population Project, which is developing methods to link historical Census data to contemporary Census data and administrative records. Sanders holds a Ph.D. in economics from the University of Chicago.

Desi Small-Rodriguez is assistant professor of sociology and American Indian studies at the University of California, Los Angeles. She has partnered with Indigenous communities in the United States and internationally as a researcher and data advocate for more than 10 years. Small-Rodriguez directs the Data Warriors Lab, an Indigenous social science laboratory. Her research examines the intersection of race, indigeneity, data, and inequality. With a focus on Indigenous futures, her current research explores the racialization of Indigenous identity and group boundary-making, Indigenous population statistics, and data for health and economic justice on Indian reservations. Small-Rodriguez is cofounder of the U.S. Indigenous Data Sovereignty Network, which helps ensure that data for and about

Indigenous nations and peoples in the United States (American Indians, Alaska Natives, and Native Hawaiians) are utilized to advance Indigenous aspirations for collective and individual well-being. She also serves on the board of directors for the Missing and Murdered Indigenous Women's Database. Small-Rodriguez received her Ph.D. in sociology from the University of Arizona.

David T. Takeuchi is associate dean for faculty excellence in the University of Washington School of Social Work. He is a sociologist with extensive experience in research design, sampling strategies for diverse populations, and data analyses using different statistical methods; he has written extensively on issues related to the unequal distribution of health and illness in society, particularly around race, ethnic, immigration, and socioeconomic status. Takeuchi received the Legacy Award from the Family Research Consortium for his research and mentoring and the Innovations Award from the National Center on Health and Health Disparities for his research contributions. He received the University of Washington 2011 Marsha Landolt Distinguished Mentor Award, the Leonard Pearlin Award for Distinguished Contributions of the Sociological Study of Health, and the American Sociological Association's Award for Distinguished Contributions to the Study of Asian American Communities. Takeuchi is an elected member of the Washington State Academy of Sciences, the Sociological Research Association, and the American Academy of Social Work and Social Welfare, and he is a current member of the National Academies of Sciences, Engineering, and Medicine's Committee on Population. He received his Ph.D. in sociology from the University of Hawaii.